ELON MUSK
A COMPLETE BIOGRAPHY

The Logos used on Cover are owned by

Tesla and SpaceX

ABHISHEK KUMAR

Published by

PRABHAT PRAKASHAN PVT. LTD.
4/19 Asaf Ali Road,
New Delhi-110 002 (INDIA)
e-mail: prabhatbooks@gmail.com

ISBN 978-93-5521-134-7
ELON MUSK A COMPLETE BIOGRAPHY
by Abhishek Kumar

Edition
2026

Price
₹ 300 (Rupees Three Hundred Only)

Printed at
R-Tech Offset Printers, Delhi

Contents

When Musk Met Modi

In the year 2015, when Narendra Modi, after being elected as India's Prime Minister visited the United States of America, he paid a visit to the Tesla factory. He visited the facilities of Tesla Motors in San Jose, California. PM Modi showed obvious interest in several inventions and concepts of the company, but his primary interest was in the company's solar Powerwall technology. Modi and Musk also discussed the probability of a more inexpensive car from the company.

Powerwall uses a rechargeable lithium-ion battery to stock power during the daytime when needs are small, or by using solar panels throughout the middle of the day when the sun is at its peak point; and then discharging it for home use when the rates are higher, thus causing in bigger savings and a lesser adverse effect on the environment.

The technology decreases the reliance on the electricity grid for metropolitan homes, and Modi was impressed by the potential of the Powerwall which could be very effective in the rural areas of India, especially to help farmers. The two also discussed novel machinery being advanced for both motorised and energy areas by Tesla Motors that can have noteworthy affirmative consequences in emerging economies, particularly after recent government initiatives such as the FAME (Faster Adoption and Manufacturing of Electric Vehicles) scheme.

❑

The Future We are Building and Boring

•

In an interview given to TED's Head Curator, Chris Anderson on 3rd May, 2017, Elon Musk talks about Tesla and SpaceX and his motivation for building a future on Mars. The talk between the two gives an interesting insight of Musk's style of functioning and thinking. Below is a transcription of the interview.

Chris: Elon. Hey, welcome back to TED. It's great to have you here.

Elon: Thanks for having me.

Chris: So, in the next half an hour or so we're going to spend some time exploring your vision for what an exciting future might look like, which I guess makes my first question a little ironic. Why are you boring?

Elon: Yeah. I ask myself that frequently. We're trying to dig a hole under L.A., and this is to create the beginning of what will hopefully be a 3-D network of tunnels to alleviate congestion. So, I mean right now, one of the most soul-destroying things is traffic. It affects people in every part of the world. It takes away so much of your life. It's… it's horrible. It's particularly horrible in L.A. and…

Chris: I think you've brought with you the first visualisation that's been shown of this. Can I show this?

Elon: Yeah absolutely. So this is the first time. Just sort of show what we're talking about. So a couple of key things those are important in having a 3D tunnel network. First of all, you have to be able to integrate the entrance and exit of the tunnel seamlessly into the fabric of the city. So by having an elevator, sort of a car skate that's on an elevator, you can integrate the entrances and exits to the tunnel network just by using two parking spaces. And then the car gets on a skate. There's no speed limit here. So we're designing this to be able to operate 200 kilometers, about 130 miles.

Chris: What?

Elon: 200 kilometers an hour or about 130 miles per hour. So you should be able to get from say Westwood to LAX in six minutes. Five, to six minutes.

Applause

Chris: So possibly, initially done, it's like on a sort of toll road type basis.

Elon: Yeah.

Chris: Which I guess alleviate some traffic from the surface streets as well.

Elon: So I don't know if you notice in the video, but there's no real limit to how many levels of the tunnel you can have. You can go much further deep than you can go up. The deepest mines are much deeper than the tallest buildings are tall so that you can alleviate any arbitrary level of urban congestion with a 3D home network. This is a very important point. So a key rebuttal to the tunnels is that if you add one layer of tunnels, then that will simply alleviate congestion, it will get used up, and then you'll be back where you started, back with congestion. But you can go to any arbitrary number of tunnels any number of levels.

Chris: But people, seen traditionally it's incredibly expensive to dig, and that would block this idea.

Elon: Yeah. Well, they're right. To give an example, the LA subway extension, which is, I think it's a two-and-a-half mile extension that was just completed for two billion dollars. So roughly, a billion dollars a mile to do the subway extension in LA and this is not the highest utility subway in the world. So, yeah, it's quite difficult to dig tunnels normally. I think we need to have at least a tenfold 10-fold improvement in the cost per mile of tunnelling.

Chris: And how could you achieve that?

Elon: I guess actually if you just do two things you can get to approximately an order of magnitude improvement. And I think you can go beyond that. So the first thing to do is to cut the total tunnel diameter by a factor of two or more. So it's a single road lane tunnel according to regulations has to be 26 feet maybe 28 feet in diameter to allow for crashes and emergency vehicles and sufficient ventilation for a combustion engine cars. But if you shrink that diameter to what we were attempting which is 12 feet, which is plenty to get an electric skate through, you drop the diameter by a factor of two and the cross-sectional area by a factor of four and the tunnelling costs scale with the cross-sectional area. So that's roughly a half order of magnitude improvement right there. Then tunnelling machines currently tunnel for half the time then they stop, and then the rest of the time is putting in reinforcements for the tunnel wall. So if you design the machine instead to do continuous tunnelling and to reinforce, that will give you a factor of two improvements. Combine that, and it's a factor of eight. Also, these machines are far from being at their power or thermal limits so that you can jack up the power to the machine substantially. I think you can get at least a factor of two, maybe a factor of four or five improvements on the on top of that. So I think that, there's a fairly straightforward series of steps to get somewhere more than an order of magnitude improvement in the cost per mile. And our target is, we've got a pet snail called Gary, this is from Gary the snail from "South Park", I mean, sorry, Sponge Bob Square Pants". So Gary is as capable of.... Currently, he's capable of going 14 times faster than a tunnel-boring machine. OK.

Laughter in the audience

Chris: You want to beat Gary.

Elon: We want to beat Gary. Yeah yeah. He's not a patient little fellow. And we want to. That will be a victory. Victory is beating the snail.

Chris: But a lot of people imagining, dreaming about future cities, they imagine that actually, the solution is sort of flying cars, drones, etcetera. You go above ground. Why isn't that a better solution? You save all that tunnelling cost.

Elon: Right. I'm in favour of flying things. Obviously, I do rockets, so I like things that fly. This is not some inherent bias against flying things, but there is a challenge with flying cars in that they will be quite noisy. The wind force generated will be very high. They just… Let's just say that if something is flying over your head. There is a whole bunch of flying cars going all over the place. That is not an anxiety-reducing situation. You don't think to yourself, "Well, I feel better about today." You're thinking like, "Did they service their hubcap or is it going to come off and guillotine me?" Things like that.

Chris: So you see this vision of future cities with this rich 3D network of tunnels underneath. Is there a tie-in here with Hyperloop? Could you apply these tunnels to use for this Hyperloop idea you had, you had released a few years ago?

Elon: Yes, so…you know we've been puttering around with the Hyperloop stuff for a while. We built a Hyperloop test track adjacent to SpaceX, just for student competition, to encourage innovative ideas in transport. And it actually, ends up being the biggest vacuum chamber in the world after the Large Hadron Collider, by volume. So it's quite fun to do that, but it was a hobby thing, and then we think we might. We developed a little pusher car to push these student pods. But we're going to try seeing how fast we can make the pusher go if it's not pushing something. So I mean, we are cautiously optimistic that we'll be able to be faster than the world's fastest bullet train even in a 0.8-mile stretch.

Chris: Wow. Good brakes.

Elon: Yeah, I mean it's either going to smash into tiny pieces or go quite fast.

Chris: You can picture then, a Hyperloop in a tunnel running quite long distances.

Elon: Yes. Exactly. So in looking at tunnelling technology, it turns out that to make a tunnel, you have to seal against the water table, you've got to typically design a tunnel wall to be good to about five or six atmospheres. So to go to vacuum is only one atmosphere, or near vacuum. So actually, it sorts of turns out that automatically, if you build a tunnel that is good enough to resist the water table, it's automatically capable of holding vacuum. So yeah.

Chris: So you can picture, what kind of length tunnel is in Elon's future to running Hyperloop?

Elon: I think there's no there's no real length limit. You could dig as much as you want. I think as if you were to do something like D.C. to New York Hyperloop, I think you'd probably want to go underground the entire way because it's a high-density area. You're going to a lot of buildings and houses. And if you go deep enough, you cannot detect the tunnel. And this is so many people think well it's going to be pretty annoying to have a tunnel dug under my house. Like, if that tunnel is dug more than about three or four tunnel diameters beneath your house, you will not be able to detect it being dug at all. In fact, if you're able to detect the tunnel being dug, whatever device you are using, you can get a lot of money for that device from the Israeli military, who is trying to detect tunnels from Hamas, and from the U.S. Customs and Border Patrol that try to detect drug tunnels. So if you. The reality is that the Earth is incredibly good at absorbing the vibrations, and once the tunnel depth is below a certain level, it is undetectable. Maybe you have a very sensitive seismic instrument you might be able to detect it.

Chris: So you started a new company to do this called The Boring Company. Very nice, very funny.

Elon: What's funny about that?

Chris: How much of your time is this?

Elon: It's maybe two or three percent.

Chris: So you've bought a hobby. This is what an Elon Musk hobby looks like.

Elon: I mean, it is like, we…. You know this is basically interns and people doing it part-time. So this is like, we bought, you know, some second-hand machinery and it's just, it's puttering along, but it's making good progress so….

Chris: So an even bigger part of your time is being spent on electrifying cars and transport through Tesla. Is one of the motivations for that for the tunnelling project, the realisation that actually in a world where cars are electric and where they're self-driving, there may end up being more cars on the roads on any given hour than there are now?

Elon: Yeah exactly. A lot of people think that once, when you make cars autonomous, that they'll be able to go faster and that will alleviate congestion. And to some degree that will be true. But once you have shared autonomy where it's much cheaper to go by car, and you can go point to point, the affordability of going in a car will be will be better than that of a bus. Like, it would cost less than a bus ticket. So the amount of driving that will occur will be much greater with shared autonomy, and actually, traffic will get far worse.

Chris: You started Tesla with the goal of persuading the world to accept that electrification was the future of cars. And a few years ago, people were laughing at you. Now not so much. I mean…

Elon: Ok.

Laughter

Elon: I don't know. I don't know.

Chris: But isn't it true that pretty much every auto manufacturer has announced serious electrification plans for the short- to medium-term future?

Elon: Yeah, yeah. I think almost every automaker has some electric vehicle program. They vary in seriousness. Some are very serious about transitioning entirely too electric, and some are just dabbling in it. And some, amazingly, are still pursuing fuel cells, but I think that won't last much longer.

Chris: But isn't there a sense, though, Elon, where you could now just declare victory and say, you know,

"We did it." Let the world electrify, and you go on and focus on other stuff?

Elon: Yeah. I intend to stay with Tesla as far into the future as I can imagine. And there are a lot of exciting things that we have coming. We've got the Model 3. It's coming soon. We'll be unveiling the Tesla Semi-Truck and….

Chris: Ok. We're going come to this. The Model 3. It's coming. It's supposed to be coming in July.

Elon: Yeah it's looking quite good for starting production in July.

Chris: Wow. One of the things that people are excited about is the fact that it's got autopilot and you put out this video a while back showing what that technology looks like or would look like. There's obviously an autopilot in Model S right now.

Elon: Yeah

Chris: What do we see here?

Elon: Yes, this is using only cameras and a GPS. So no LIDAR or radar is being used here. This is just using passive optical, which is essentially, what a person uses. The whole road system is meant to be navigated with passive optical cameras. And so once you solve camera's vision, then autonomy is solved. If you don't solve vision, it's not solved. So that's why our focus is so heavily on having a vision neural net that's very effective for road conditions.

Chris: Right. Many other people are going the LIDAR route. You want cameras plus radar as most of it.

Elon: You can absolutely be superhuman with just cameras. Like, you could probably do 10 times better than humans would, with just, cameras.

Chris: So the new cars being sold right now have eight cameras in them. They can't yet do, what that camera showed. When will they be able to?

Elon: I think that we're still on track for being able to go cross-country from LA to New York by the end of the year, fully autonomous.

Chris: So by the end of the year, you're saying, that someone is going to sit in a Tesla without touching the steering wheel. Tap in "New York", off it goes.

Elon: Yeah.

Chris: Won't have ever to touch the wheel. By the end of 2017.

Elon: Yeah essentially November or December of this year, we should be able to go from all the way from a parking lot in California to a parking lot in New York. No controls touched at any point during the entire journey.

Applause

Chris: Amazing. Part of that is possible because you've already got a fleet of Teslas driving all these roads. You're accumulating a huge amount of data of national road system.

Elon: Yes. But the thing that was interesting is that I'm fairly confident it will be able to do that route even if you change the route dynamically. So it gets fairly easy.... If you say I'm going to be good at one specific route, that's one thing, but it should be able to go, really be very good, so once you enter a highway, to go anywhere on the highway system in a given country. It's not sort of limited to LA or New York. We could we could change and make it. Seattle, Florida that day, or you know, in real time. So you are going from L.A. to New York now go from L.A. to Toronto.

Chris: So leaving aside regulation for a second, regarding the technology alone, the time when someone will be able to buy one of your cars and literally just take the hands of the wheel and go to sleep and wake up and find that they've arrived. How far away is that? To do that safely?

Elon: That's about two years. So the real trick of it is not in how you make it work say 99.9 percent of the time, because if a car crashes, say one in a thousand times, then you're probably still not going to be comfortable falling asleep. You know, you shouldn't be, certainly. But, it's not going to be. It's never going to be perfect. No system is going to be perfect. But you say it's perhaps; the car is unlikely to crash in a hundred lifetimes or a thousand lifetimes, then people like, OK, wow, if I would live a thousand lives, I would still most likely never experienced a crash, then that's probably OK.

Chris: To sleep, I guess a big concern of yours is that people get seduced too early to think that this is safe.

Elon: Yeah

Chris: And that you'll have some horrible incident happen that put things back.

Elon: Well, I think that the autonomy system is likely to at least mitigate the crash except in rare circumstances, but the thing to appreciate about vehicle safety is this is probabilistic. I mean, there is some chance that any time a human driver gets in the car, that they will have an accident that is their fault. It's never zero. And so really the key threshold for autonomy is how much better is autonomy need to be that a person before you can rely on it.

Chris: But once you get that literally safe hands-off driving, the power to disrupt the whole industry seems massive, because at that point you've spoken of people being able to buy, car drops off work, and then you let it go and provide a sort of Uber-like service to other people, earn you money, maybe even cover the cost of the lease of that car.

Elon: Exactly

Chris: So you get a car for free. Is that likely?

Elon: Yeah absolutely, this is what will happen. So there will be a shared autonomy fleet where you buy your car, and you can choose to use that car exclusively. You can choose to have used only by friends and family only by five stars...other drivers who are rated five stars. You can choose to share it sometimes but not other times. That's 100 percent what will occur. It's just a question of when.

Chris: Wow. So you mentioned the Semi, and I think you're planning to announce this in September, but I'm curious whether there's anything you could show us today?

Elon: I will show you a teaser shot of the truck. It's alive.

Chris: OK.

Elon: Now this is definitely a case we want to be cautious about the autonomy features because—

Chris: We can't see that much of it. It doesn't look like just a little friendly neighbourhood truck. It looks kind of badass. What sort of semi is this?

Elon: So this is a heavy duty, long range, semi-truck. So it's like the highest weight capability and with long range. So essentially, it's meant to alleviate the heavy-duty trucking loads. And this is something, which people do not today think is possible. They think the truck doesn't have enough power or it doesn't have enough range. And then with those with the Tesla semi, we want to show that no, an electric truck actually can out-torque any diesel semi and if you had a tug-of-war competition, the Tesla semi what will tug the diesel semi uphill.

Laughter

Chris: That's pretty cool. And short term these aren't driverless? These are going to be trucks that truck drivers want to drive.

Elon: Yes. So what will be really fun about this is you have a flat torque RPM curve with an electric motor, whereas with a diesel motor or any kind of internal combustion engine car you've got a torque RPM curve that looks like a hill. So this will be a very spry truck. You could drive this around like a sports car. There are no gears. It's like a single speed.

Chris: So, there is a great movie to be made here somewhere. I don't know what it is, and I don't know that it ends well, but there is a great movie.

Elon: I mean it's quite a bizarre test-driving. You know, when I was driving the test prototype for the first truck, it's really weird because you're driving around and you're just you're so nimble, and you're in this giant truck.

Chris: Wait, wait. You've already driven the prototype.

Elon: Yeah, yeah. I drove it around the parking lot. I was like this is crazy.

Chris: Wow. This is no vaporware.

Elon: It is just like driving this giant truck and sort of making these mad manoeuvres.

Chris: This is cool. OK, from a really badass picture to a kind of less badass picture. This is just a cute house from "Desperate Housewives" or something. What on earth is going on here?

Elon: Well this illustrates the picture of the future that I think is how things will evolve. You've got an electric car in the driveway. If you look in between the electric car and the house, there are actually three power walls stacked up against the side of the house, and then that house roof is a solar roof. So that's the actual solar glass roof.

Chris: OK. So those…

Elon: That's a picture of a real, well…admittedly it's a real fake house. That's a real fake house.

Chris: So this are these roof tiles. Some of them have in them…

Elon: Yeah.

Chris: Basically solar power. The ability to…

Elon: Yeah. Solar glass tiles where you can you can adjust the texture and the colour to a very fine grain level. And then there's micro louvres in the glass, such that when you're looking at the roof from street level or close to street level. All the tiles look the same whether there is a solar panel behind it or a solar cell behind it or not. So you have an even colour from the ground level. If you look at it from a helicopter, you're actually able to look through and see that some of the glass tiles have a solar cell behind them and some do not. You can't tell from street level.

Chris: Right. You put them in the ones that are likely to see a lot of suns, and that makes them super affordable, right. Not that much more expensive than just tiling the roof.

Elon: Yeah, we're very confident that the cost of the roof plus the cost of electricity… A solar glass roof will be less than the cost of a normal roof plus the cost of electricity. So in other words, this will be economically, a no-brainer. It will look…. We think it will look great…. And it will last…. We thought about having the warranty be infinity, but then people said, well, that might sound like we were just talking rubbish, but I actually this is toughened glass. Well after the house has collapsed and there's nothing there, the roof…the glass tiles will still be there.

Chris: I mean this is cool. So you're rolling this out in a couple of weeks' time, I think with four different roofing types.

Elon: Yeah, we're starting off with two. Two initially and the second two will be introduced early next year.

Chris: What's the scale of ambition here? How many houses do you believe could end up having this type of roofing?

Elon: I mean, I think eventually. I think eventually almost all houses will have a solar roof. Now the thing is to consider the time scale here to be probably on the order of 40 or 50 years. So on average, the roof is replaced every 20 to 25 years. So but you don't you don't start replacing all roofs immediately, but eventually, if you say you were to fast forward to say 15 years from now, it will be unusual to have a roof that does not have solar.

Chris: Is there a mental model thing that people don't get here that is been because of the shift in the cost, the economics of solar power that like most houses actually have enough sunlight on their roof, pretty much to power all of their needs if you could capture the power. You could pretty much power all that needs right? But you could go off with the kind of grid?

Elon: Yeah. It kind of depends on where you are and what the house size is relative to the roof area. But it's a fair statement to say that most houses in the United States have enough roof area to power all the needs of the house.

Chris: OK. So the key to the economics of the cars, the Semi, these houses, is the falling price of lithium-ion batteries, which you have made a huge bet on as Tesla and in many ways, that's the core competency. And you've decided to really, like, own that competency; you just have to build the world's largest manufacturer to double the world's supply of lithium-ion batteries.

Elon: Yeah.

Chris: With this guy. What is this?

Elon: Yes, so that's the Gigafactory, the progress so far on the Gigafactory. Eventually, you could sort of roughly see that there's sort of a diamond shape overall. When it's fully done, it'll be it looks like a giant diamond or that's the idea behind it. It's aligned on true North. That's a small detail.

Chris: And capable of producing like one hundred or eventually like a hundred 100-gigawatt hours of the batteries a year.

Elon: A hundred 100-gigawatt hours. We think probably more, but yeah.

Chris: And they're actually being produced right now. Right. This is the video, I mean is that speeded up.

Elon: That's actually the slowed down version.

Chris: Yeah. How fast does it actually go?

Elon: Well when it's running at full speed, you can't actually see the cells without a strobe light. It just blurs.

Chris: I mean one of your one of your core ideas, Elon, about what makes an exciting future is a future where we no longer feel guilty about energy. How? Help us picture this. I mean how many Gigafactories if you like, does it take to get us there.

Elon: It's about a hundred roughly. It's not ten. It is not a thousand. Most likely a hundred.

Chris: I kind of find this amazing. You can actually picture, if that's right, you can picture what it would take to move the world of this vast fossil fuel thing. It's like you're building one. Cost 5 billion dollars maybe the next one or whatever, $5–to 10 billion dollars. Like it's kind of cool that you can picture that project. And you're planning to do, at Tesla or at least announce another two this year.

Elon: I will announce locations for between two and four Gigafactories later this year probably four.

Chris: Wow.

Applause

Chris: No more teasing from you for here. Like where? Continents. You can say no.

Elon: We need to address a global market.

Chris: OK this is cool. Hehe. I think we should actually double mark it, so I have to ask you one question about politics, only one. I'm kind of sick of politics, but I do want to ask you this. You're on a body now advising a guy who has said he doesn't really believe in climate change and there's a lot of people out there who kind of think you shouldn't be doing that. They'd like you to walk away from that. What would you say to them?

Elon: Well I think that this first of all I'm just on two advisory councils where the format consists of going around the room and asking people's opinion on things. And so there's like a meeting every month or two. You know that's the sum total of my contribution. But I think to the degree that there are people in the room who are arguing in favour of doing something about climate change or, you know, another sort of social issues. You know, I mean, I've used the meetings I've had thus far to argue in favour of immigration and favour of climate change and if I hadn't done that, there wouldn't be that, what wasn't on the agenda before. So maybe nothing will happen, but at least the words were said.

Chris: OK. So, let's talk SpaceX and Mars. Last time you were here, you spoke about what seemed like a kind of incredibly ambitious dream to develop rockets that are actually reusable. And you've only gone and done it.

Elon: Yeah. Finally. It took a long time.

Chris: Talk us through this. What are we looking at here?

Elon: This is one of our rocket boosters coming back from very high and fast in space. So just delivered the upper stage at high velocity. I think this may have been sort of Mark 7 or so. Delivery of the upper stage.

Chris: That was sped up…

Elon: That's the slowed down version.

Chris: I thought that was the sped-up version. But, I mean, that's amazing. And several of these failed before you finally figured out how to get to do it. But now you've landed, you've done this what five or six times?

Elon: eight, nine, or something.

Chris: Yeah. And for the first time, re-flown one of the rockets that landed so….

Elon: Yeah, we landed the rocket booster and then prepped it for flight again and flew it again. It's the first re-flight of an orbital booster where that re-flight is relevant, so it's important to appreciate that reusability is only relevant if it is rapid and complete.

Chris: Right.

Elon: So like an aircraft or a car, the reusability is rapid and complete. You do not send your aircraft into Boeing in between flights.

Chris: Right. So this is allowing you to dream of this really ambitious idea of sending like many, many people to Mars in 10 or 20 years' time, I guess. In the next 20 years.

Elon: Yeah.

Chris: And you've designed this outrageous rocket to do it. Help us understand the scale of this thing.

Elon: Well visually, you can see that's a person. That and that's the vehicle.

Chris: So if that was a skyscraper. That's like a 40 stories high skyscraper.

Elon: Yeah. Probably a little more. Yeah. The thrust level of this is really…. This configuration is about four times the thrust of the Saturn V moon rocket.

Chris: Four times the thrust of the biggest rocket humanity ever created before.

Elon: Yeah, yeah. I mean….

Chris: As one does

Elon: Yeah.

Laughter

Elon: I mean in units of 747, a 747 is only about a quarter million pounds of thrust. So that's. So there are probably 10 million pounds of thrust there's 40, 747's. So, this would be the thrust equivalent of 120, 747's, with all engines blazing.

Chris: And so even with a machine designed to escape Earth's gravity, I think you told me last time, this thing can actually take a fully loaded 747, people, cargo, everything into orbit?

Elon: Exactly. This thing can take a fully loaded 747 with maximum fuel, maximum passengers, maximum cargo on the 747. This can take it as cargo.

Chris: So based on this you presented recently this Interplanetary Transport System, which is visualised this way, and this is a scene you picture in, what, 30 years or, 20 years time? People are walking into this rocket.

Elon: I mean I'm hopeful it's sort of in the eight… Eight to the ten-year time frame. Aspirationally that's our target. Our internal targets are more aggressive. But I think. Yeah. So this seems quite large, and it's large by comparison with other rockets. I think…. The future spacecraft will make this look like a rowboat. I mean this is. The future spaceships will be truly enormous.

Chris: Why, Elon. Because of this…Why do we need to build a city on Mars with a million people on it in your lifetime, which I think is kind of, what you've said you'd love to do?

Elon: Yeah, I think it's important to have a future that is inspiring and appealing. I mean, I just think that there have to be reasons that you get up in the morning and you want to live. Like why do you want to live? What's the point? What inspires you? What do you love about the future? And if we're not out there. If the future does not include being out there among the stars and being a multi-planet species, I find that's incredibly depressing if that's not the future that we're going to have.

Applause

Chris: People want what position this as an either or. That there are so many desperate things happening on the planet now from climate to poverty. You know you pick your issue, and this feels like a distraction. You shouldn't be thinking about this. You should be solving what's here now. And to be fair, you've done a fair old bit to actually do that with you, you know, work on sustainable energy. But why not just do that?

Elon: I think there's. I look at the future from the standpoint of probabilities. It's like it's like a branching stream of probabilities. And their actions that we can take that affect those probabilities. Or that accelerate one thing or slow down another thing, or make you know, introduce something new to the probability stream. Sustainable energy will happen no matter what. If there was no Tesla. If Tesla would have never existed, it would have to happen out of necessity. It is tautological. If you don't have sustainable energy, it means you have unsustainable energy. Eventually, you run out, and the laws of economics will drive or drive civilisation towards sustainable energy inevitably. The fundamental value of a company like Tesla is the degree to which it accelerates the advent of sustainable energy. Faster than it would otherwise occur.

So I think like what is the fundamental good of a company like Tesla, I would say, hopefully, if it accelerated that by a decade, potentially more than a decade, that would be quite a good thing to occur. That's what I consider to be the fundamental sort of aspirational good of Tesla.

Then, there's becoming a multi-planet species and space-faring civilisation. This is not inevitable. It's very important to appreciate this is not inevitable. The sustainable energy future, I think, is largely inevitable but being a space-faring civilisation is definitely not inevitable. If you look at the progress in space, in 1969, we were able to send somebody to the moon. 1969. Then we had the Space Shuttle. The Space Shuttle could only take people to low Earth orbit. Then the Space Shuttle retired, and the United States could take no one to orbit.

So that's the trend. The trend is like down to nothing. This is not… We're mistaken when we think that technology just automatically improves. It does not automatically improve. It only improves if a lot of people work very hard to make it better. And actually it will, I think, it by itself degrade actually. We look at great civilisations like ancient Egypt, and they were able to make the pyramids, and they forgot how to do that. And the Romans they built these incredible aqueducts. They forgot how to do it.

Chris: You know, it almost seems listening to you and looking at all the different things you've done, that you've got this unique double motivation on everything that I find so interesting. One is this desire to work for humanity's long-term good. The other is the desire to do something exciting. And it often feels like you, you feel like, you need the one to drive the other. With Tesla, you want to have sustainable energy, so you make these super sexy, exciting cars to do it. You know, solar energy, we need to get there, so we need to make these beautiful roofs. We haven't even spoken about your newest thing, which we don't have time to do, but you want to save humanity from bad AI, and so you're going to create this really cool brain-machine interface to give us all infinite memory and telepathy and so forth. And on Mars, it feels like what you're saying is, yeah we need we need to save humanity and have a backup plan, but also we need to inspire humanity. And this is this is a way to inspire.

Elon: I think that the value of using inspiration is very much underrated. No question. But I want to be clear; I am not trying to be anyone's saviour. That is not the point. I'm just trying to think about the future and not be sad.

Chris: Beautiful statement. I think everyone here would agree that it is not. None of this is going to happen inevitably. The fact that in your mind, you dream this stuff. You dream stuff that no one else would dare dream or no one else would be capable of dreaming at the level of complexity that you do. The fact that you do that, Elon Musk, is a really remarkable thing. Thank you for helping us all to dream a bit bigger.

Elon: But you'll tell me if it ever starts getting genuinely insane right?

Laughter & Applause

Chris: Thank you, Elon Musk. That was really, really fantastic. That was really fantastic.

❑

Introduction

As Ashlee Vance, Elon Musk's biographer was waiting for him in a restaurant; Musk showed up. He was about fifteen 15 minutes late and was wearing leather shoes, designer jeans, and a plaid dress shirt. He stands six foot one, but Vance says that he seems much bigger than that. Vance describes him as absurdly broad-shouldered, sturdy, and thick. He describes his body posture as, 'to be almost sheepish.'

But to understand Musk well, one must start with the headquarters of SpaceX, in Hawthorne, California—at the outskirts of Los Angeles, a few miles from Los Angeles International Airport. There one can find two huge posters of Mars hanging side by side on the wall leading up to Musk's workspace. The picture on the left paints Mars as it is today—a cold, desolated red planet. The other one on the right displays a Mars with a gigantic green mainland enclosed by oceans. The planet has been heated up and transformed to suit humans. Musk plans to make this happen. Turning humans into space colonisers is his life's stated purpose. "If we can solve sustainable energy and be well on our way to becoming a multi-planetary species with a self-sustaining civilisation on another planet—to cope with a worst-case scenario happening and extinguishing human consciousness—then," he continues, "I think that would be good." Musk's disposition to challenge difficult things has made him a deity in Silicon Valley, where colleagues CEOs like Page speak of him in admiration, and nascent moguls struggle "to be like Elon".

In 2012, SpaceX flew a supply capsule to the International Space Station and brought it safely back to Earth. Moreover, Tesla Motors carried the Model S- — an attractive, all-electric sedan that took the locomotive industry's breath away and clouted Detroit. The two feats raised up Musk's stature to the rarest heights among industry's titans. Apart from Steve Jobs, who could claim similar achievements in two such different industries, Musk was unbeatable. But he is not done yet. He is also the chairman and the biggest stockholder of Solar City, a thriving solar energy establishment poised to file for an initial public offering.

SpaceX has its headquarters at Hawthorne. It's an unwelcoming part of Los Angeles District in which groups of dilapidated houses, ramshackle shops, and shabby eateries border huge, industrial complexes. One is enthralled by the view of one 550,000-square-foot feet rectangle painted a grandiose kind of white. This is the main SpaceX building. Musk has built a rocket factory in the middle of Los Angeles. The factory is a giant, shared work area. At the back are delivery bays that allow for the arrival of chunks of metal, which are related to high-welding machines. On one side are the technicians building motherboards, radios, and other electronics. Rockets line up one after the other, ready to be placed on trucks. Some rockets, in another part of the building, await coats of white paint. There are hundreds of workers in constant motion. SpaceX acquires several buildings that used to be part of a Boeing factory.

The 1990s were the times of the internet bubble in the United States. Everyone seemed to be in the rush of trying to find that next big thing in the dot-com world.

It was the same time that Musk started working on his first project after finishing college, company called Zip2. It ended up as a big and quick success. Compaq bought Zip2 in 1999 for $307 million. Musk earned $22 million from the deal and emptied almost all of it into his next undertaking, a start-up that would transform into PayPal. Being the biggest shareholder in PayPal, Musk became extremely rich when eBay acquired the company for $1.5 billion in 2002. He then moved to Los Angeles. He invested $100 million into SpaceX, $70 million into Tesla, and $10 million into Solar City. All of Musk's firms make things from scratch and attempt to change round much that the aerospace, locomotive, and solar industries have recognised as the way to go about. With SpaceX, Musk is fighting the hulks of the U.S. military-industrial composite, counting Lockheed Martin and Boeing. He's also clashing with countries— markedly China and Russia. SpaceX has made a name for itself as the low-cost provider in the trade. Musk's foes build weapons for a living. SpaceX is testing refillable rockets that can carry cargos to space and bring it back to Earth, with precision. Once after having perfected this technology, the company will bring a devastating blow to all of its competitors and will establish the United States as the world leader in taking cargo and humans to space. With Tesla, Musk has revamped the way cars are contrived and vented while constructing out a universal energy delivery network at the same time. Tesla strives to make all-electric cars that push the limits of technology. The company doesn't sell cars through dealers but on the Web. Tesla does not make lots of money from repairing its vehicles, as its electric cars do not require the oil changes and other upkeep processes of old-style cars. 'The direct sales model' incorporated by Tesla is the key injury to car dealers used to make their incomes from excessive maintenance bills. Its recharging stations now run together with many of the main freeways in Europe, the United States, and Asia. They can add miles to a car in only about twenty 20 minutes. These stations are solar-powered, and car owners pay no money to refuel. It is a futuristic end-to-end transportation system that would change the way people drive around the world. Solar City, is the biggest installer and financer of solar panels for consumers and businesses. Musk is its chairman, while his cousins Lyndon and Peter Rive run the company. Musk is one of the richest men in the world, with a net worth around $10 billion.

He has a very hectic schedule. On Mondays, he works the whole day at SpaceX. On Tuesday, he begins at SpaceX, then flies to Silicon Valley in his jet. He spends a couple of days working at Tesla, which has its offices in Palo

Alto and factory in Fremont. Musk does not own a home in Northern California and stays at the Luxe Rosewood hotel or friends' houses. Then it's back to Los Angeles and SpaceX on Thursday. He shares custody of his five young boys—twins and triplets—with his ex-wife, Justine, and spends with them four days in a week.

In short, he's an inventor, celebrity businessman, and an industrialist and as many call him, "'our last hope.'" South Africa born Musk today is America's most groundbreaking entrepreneur, and eccentric thinker, and the person most likely to set Silicon Valley on a more aspiring course.

❑

Where It All Began

•

In 1984, the South African trade publication PC and Office Technology issued the source code to a video game Musk had designed which he had named Blaster. It was a science-fiction-inspired space game that required 167 lines of instructions to run. This coverage made Musk richer by five hundred dollars. The game was published on page 69 of the magazine. The magazine explained the game as- “In this game, you have to destroy an alien space freighter, which is carrying deadly Hydrogen Bombs and Status Beam Machines. This game makes good use of sprites and animation, and in this sense makes the listing worth reading." In his teenage, Musk variegated fantasy and reality to the point that they were hard to separate in his mind. "Maybe I read too many comics as a kid," Musk said. "In the comics, it always seems like they are trying to save the world. It seemed like one should try to make the world a better place because the inverse makes no sense."

At the young age of fourteen14, Musk turned to religious and philosophical texts. It was at this age that he came across one of the most influential books in his life: The Hitchhiker's Guide to the Galaxy, by Douglas Adams. "Once you figure out the question, then the answer is relatively easy. I concluded that we should aspire to increase the scope and scale of. He points out that one of the really tough things is figuring out what questions to ask," Musk said.

Musk was born in 1971 in Pretoria, in the north-eastern part of South Africa, an hour's drive from Johannesburg. This was the time in South Africa when tension and violence spilt on the streets. Musk turned four years old just days after the Soweto Uprising, in which hundreds of black students died while protesting decrees of the white government. What had the highest impact on Musk's personality was the white Afrikaner culture prevalent in Pretoria. Since early childhood Musk had a reserved personality and geeky inclinations. He always dreamt of moving to America and saw it as the land of opportunity and the stage for making his dreams come true. Musk reached the United States in his twenties. His ancestors having the Swiss-German last name of Haldeman on the maternal side of his family left Europe for New York in the course of the Revolutionary War. Starting in New York, they spread out to the lowlands of the Midwest like Illinois and Minnesota. His great-grandfather John Elon Haldeman, born in 1872 and grew up in Illinois and later moved to Minnesota. There he met his wife, Almeda Jane Norman. In 1902, the couple settled down in a log cabin in the central Minnesota town of Pequot. They later gave birth to their son Joshua Norman Haldeman, Musk's grandfather. Joshua was an agile, independent boy. In 1907, his family moved to Saskatchewan, and his father expired soon. Joshua was seven. He took to horseback riding, boxing, and wrestling. Haldeman organised one of Canada's first rodeos. Family photographs show Joshua clad in a pretty pair of chaps demonstrating his rope-spinning abilities. As a teen, he left home to get graduation from the Palmer School of Chiropractice in Iowa and then returned to Saskatchewan to become a planter. In the 1930s, he fell into a financial catastrophe. His five thousand acres of land was seized. His son Scott Haldeman went on to receive his chiropractic degree from the same university as his father and became one of the world's top back pain specialists. After 1934, Haldeman lived a nomadic life. He did odd jobs as a construction worker and rodeo performer before resolving down as a chiropractor. In 1948, Haldeman and Winnifred Josephine Fletcher, or Wyn, welcomed twin daughters Kaye and Maye, Musk's mother in the family. Haldeman picked up flying and bought his plane. He later penned a book with his wife named The Flying Haldeman: Pity the Poor Private Pilot.

He seemed to like to have all going for him once, in 1950, he decided to give it all away. He had come to see the Canadian administration as too intrusive and contended that the ethical appeal of Canada had started to decay. He also possessed a lust for adventure. And so, he decided to move to South Africa. In South Africa, the family settled in Pretoria. Haldeman set up a new chiropractic practice in the city. The Haldemans had a freewheeling approach to nurturing their children, which would spread over the generations to Musk. The kids were not once chastised. The children were left with the impression that they were capable of anything. They only had to make a decision and do it. Haldeman died in 1974 at the age of seventy-two while doing rehearsal touchdowns in his plane and couldn't see a wire attached to a pair of poles. The wire trapped the plane's wheels and tossed the craft, and Haldeman broke his neck. Elon was a toddler back at the time. But all through his infantile, he picked up several stories about his grandfather's adventures and sat through a myriad of slideshows that acknowledged his journeys and excursions over the wilds. "My grandmother told these tales of how they almost died several times along their journeys," Musk said. "They were flying in a plane with literally no instruments—not even a radio, and they had road maps instead of aerial maps, and some of those weren't even correct. My grandfather had this desire for adventure, exploration doing crazy things."

Maye Musk, Elon's mother, born in 1948, was considered a nerd. She liked math and science. Maye was tall with ash-blond hair, high cheekbones, and beautiful angular features. She ended up as a finalist for Miss South Africa and continued to model into her sixties, appearing on the covers of magazines like New York and Elle and in Beyoncé's music videos.

Maye and Elon's father, Errol Musk, grew up in the same neighbourhood. They met for the first time when Maye was about eleven. Errol had a crush on her for years. The two dated throughout the time at university. Errol spent about seven years seeking her hand in marriage.

The marriage was intricate from the start. She became pregnant during their honeymoon and gave birth to Elon on June 28, 1971, only nine months after her wedding. The couple pared out a decent life for themselves in Pretoria. Errol toiled as an engineer and ran large projects such as office buildings, retail complexes, residential subdivisions, and an air force base, while Musk's mother set up a practice as a dietician. A year later was born his brother Kimbal, and soon afterwards came to their sister Tosca. Elon showed all the characters of an inquisitive, active child. He selected things up easily. "He seemed to understand things quicker than the other kids," said Maye. Sometimes Elon appeared to drift off into a stupor at times. Elon's parents and doctors thought he might be deaf. Doctors elected to remove his adenoid glands. He kept right on discerning, and folks around him arbitrated that he was either impolite or really strange. At five, he found a way to lump out the world and bestow all of his devotion to a sole task. He could see images in his mind's eye.

Elon was an avid reader. From a very young age, he seemed to read ten 10 hours a day; sometimes he could go through two books in a day. He could be found in the nearest bookstore somewhere near the back, sitting on the floor and reading in a surreal state. Elon would take himself to the bookstore after the school and used to stay there for hours. “At one point, I ran out of books to read at the school library and the neighbourhood library,” Musk recalls. “This is maybe the third or fourth grade. I tried to convince the librarian to order books for me. So then, I started to read the Encyclopaedia Britannica. That was so helpful. You don’t know what you don’t know. You realise there are all these things out there.” He had a photographic memory. One could ask him about whatsoever. He just remembered it all.

He was not very athletic. Once playing outside with his siblings and cousins in the night, Elon pointed out that “dark is merely the absence of light”. His relentless desire to correct people and his rough means put off other kids and further to his feelings of loneliness. As he got grew older, Elon would have strong, warm connections to his siblings. He had an outbound nature. In his family, he ultimately took on the role of elder and chief initiator among them. The Musk family owned one of the biggest houses in Pretoria.

Years later, his parents separated and divorced within the year. His mother moved with the kids to Durban. A couple of years later, Elon decided to live with his father. His younger brother Kimbal later opted to live with his father as well. Elon has two younger half-sisters of whom he's quite protective.

After the divorce, it was Elon's grandmother who looked after him. She had a very dominant personality and was an innovative woman. She would pick him up from school, and he would hang out with her playing Scrabble. Both Elon and Kimbal went to the locations of their father's job and learnt how to lay bricks, install plumbing, fit windows, and put in electrical wiring. "There were fun moments," Elon said. Errol as a father was ultra-present and very intense. He would lecture Elon and Kimbal for three to four hours without the boys being able to respond. He gave the impression to delight in being hard on the boys. Elon tried to persuade his dad to move to America and regularly spoke about his plans of living in the United States.

At a young age of ten, Elon saw a computer for the first time, at the Sandton City Mall in Johannesburg. "There was an electronics store that mostly did hi-fi-type stuff, but then, in one corner, they started stocking a few computers, I had to have that and then hounded my father to get the computer," Musk said. Shortly he possessed a Commodore VIC-20, a widely held home device that went on trade in 1980. It had five kilobytes of memory and a workbook on the BASIC programming language.

Apart from spending time with books and his new computer, Elon often took Kimbal and his cousins Russ, Lyndon, and Peter Rive on escapades. They fiddled one year in vending Easter eggs door-to-door in the area. They were not well draped, but the boys still sold them all to their wealthy neighbours. Elon also commanded them with homespun explosives and missiles. When not conducting experiments with explosives, the boys put on coatings of the outfit and gawks and shot each other with pellet guns. Elon and Kimbal raced dirt bikes against each other. The boys even picked out a spot for video arcade, got a lease, but they had to get somebody over eighteen 18 to sign a legal paper. The boys' most bold feats were their journeys between Pretoria and Johannesburg. During the 1980s, the 35-mile train trip linking Pretoria and Johannesburg was one of the world's more unsafe trips.

During middle and high school, Elon switched about a couple of institutes. He spent eighth and ninth grades at Bryanston High School. Once Elon and Kimbal were sitting on the stairs when a boy tiptoed up behind Musk, kicked him in the head, and then pushed him down the stairs. Then a handful of boys attacked him. Elon then went to the hospital. It was about a week before he could get back to school. For years, there was no relief.

Musk spent the later phases of his schooling at Pretoria Boys High School. Musk's lack of interest in sports left him secluded in the middle of a sports fixated nation. Musk didn't have any close friends at school. During science-class debates, he rallied against fossil fuels in favour of solar power. Musk fantasised about colonising other planets in high school as well. He was selected for an experimental computer program to learn the BASIC, COBOL, and Pascal programming languages. He also tried his hands at writing stories. He aced math exams and had an incredible memory.

South Africa required military service at the time. Musk wanted to avoid joining the military. At the age of 17, Musk left for Canada. He wanted to get to the United States as soon as possible and could use Canada as a stop and then make use of his Canadian lineage. He studied at the University of Pretoria for five months before heading off. He soon dropped out. The time at university went past as he awaited his Canadian documentation. His early leaning toward computers and machinery had nurtured a strong curiosity in Silicon Valley.

It took him a year to get the approvals from the Canadian government.

❑

Escape to Canada

•

In Canada, Musk knew an uncle in Montreal. Hence, he took a flight for Montreal. After reaching in June 1988, he searched for a pay phone looked for directory assistance to look for his uncle. But it didn't work. He then called his mother. She had sent a letter to the uncle before Musk left and received a reply that the uncle had gone to Minnesota. Now Musk had nowhere to stay. He headed for a youth hostel. His mother had family members dispersed all through Canada, and Musk started reaching out to them. He headed to Saskatchewan, the past home of his grandfather. He then called a second cousin and went to his house. He spent the next year doing odd jobs around the country. He looked after vegetables, and scooped out grain bins, and learnt to cut logs with a chainsaw. He also did a gig cleaning the boiler room of a lumber mill for $18 eighteen dollars an hour. Sometime later Kimbal and Elon reunited in Canada. Elon enrolled himself at Queen's University in Kingston, Ontario, in 1989.

The brothers soon made friends with the head of marketing for the Toronto Blue Jays baseball team, a business writer for the Globe and Mail, and a top executive at the Bank of Nova Scotia, Peter Nicholson. Nicholson offered Elon a summer internship at the bank and became his trusted advisor. Soon after their first meeting, Elon invited Peter Nicholson's daughter Christie to his birthday party. They never dated, but Christie found Musk interesting. The two stayed in touch during Musk's time in Canada. A pro founder affiliation arose between Musk and Justine Wilson, a fellow student at Queen's. Musk spotted Wilson on campus and went right to work trying to date her. Justine agreed to his proposal for an ice cream date. The two attended the same classes and matched their grades following an exam. At university, the two were off and on.

Navaid Farooq, a Canadian who grew up in Geneva, was Musk's classmate. The two were put in the international unit where a Canadian student was paired with a student from abroad. Musk theoretically counted as a Canadian but knew nothing about Canada. He had a roommate from Hong Kong. For some time, Musk vended computer parts and PCs in the dormitory to earn some extra cash. He would shape something that suited students' needs like a gaming machine or a simple word processor or fixes the virus. Farooq and Musk bonded soon over their common interest in board games. At college, Musk studied business, competed in public speaking contests, and began to display strength and keenness.

In 1992, after having spent two years at Queen's, Musk moved to the University of Pennsylvania on a scholarship where he went on to pursue dual degrees—one, an economics degree from the Wharton School and second, a bachelor's degree in physics. Justine stayed at Queen's and upheld a long-distance relationship with Musk.

Musk thrived even more at Penn and started to feel at ease while hanging out with his fellow physics students. Musk did not make many friends except for some and one very close friend named Adeo Ressi. Ressi went on to be a Silicon Valley entrepreneur. Both Musk and Ressi were placed in the trendy freshman dorm. The dreary social scene did not interest Ressi, and he talked Musk into letting a large house off campus. During the week, the two would study, but on the weekend, it would transmute into a nightclub. They would have as many as five 500 people and would charge five $5dollars. Musk used to have the vodka and Diet Coke but did not care for the taste of liquor.

Musk was paying his way through college and could make an entire month's rent in one night. His long time interest in solar power and in finding new ways to harness energy grew at Penn. In December 1994, Musk wrote a paper titled "The Importance of Being Solar." The document started with: "The sun will come out tomorrow. . . ." The paper foretold a rise in solar power technology centred on resources improvements and the construction of large-scale solar plants. Musk investigated intensely into how solar cells function and the numerous composites that can render them more effective. He finished the paper with a sketch of the "power station of the future." He scored 98 in the paper. His second paper spoke about taking study documents and books and electronically scanning them, and the third paper dwelled on ultra-capacitors. Directing to the newest study coming out of a lab in Silicon Valley, he wrote "The result signifies the first new means of storing significant amounts of electrical energy since the development of the battery and fuel cell. Furthermore, because the Ultra ultra-capacitor retains the basic properties of a capacitor, it can deliver its energy over one hundred times faster than a battery of equivalent weight, and be recharged just as quickly."

As he began thinking seriously about what to do after college, he temporarily reflected upon getting into the video game commerce. "I like computer games, but then if I made great computer games, how much effect would that have on the world. It wouldn't have a big effect. Even though I have an intrinsic love of video games, I couldn't bring myself to do that as a career" says Musk. He used to daydream at Queen's and Penn and concluded that the Internet, renewable energy, and space are the three regions that would experience an important change in the years to come and as the markets where he could make a big impact. He was different from the run-of-the-mill businessperson in Silicon Valley. He wasn't just sniffing out trends, and the idea of getting rich didn't consume him. He had always wanted to put a positive impact on the world and to leave it a better place for the coming generation. His sensitivity towards environment and understanding of it is what sets him apart from the rest of the lot.

❑

The Start of Start-Ups

•

In 1994, Elon, along with his brother, Kimbal, set off on a road journey through the United States of America. Kimbal had been running a small business, functioning as a franchisee for College Pro Painters. He traded off the franchise and with the money bought a 1970s BMW 320i. The brothers started their journey near San Francisco in August. They first reached Needles, a city in the Mojave Desert. The Net had recently started to become available to the common public with the help of websites like Yahoo and Netscape's browser. The brothers thought of starting a company together, something on the Web. All through the journey, they took turns driving and brainstorming. One of the ideas that arose was that of an online network for doctors to exchange information and collaborate. Kimbal went to work on a business plan and the sales and marketing side of it, but it didn't take off. During his time at Silicon Valley, Musk had worked as an intern at Pinnacle Research Institute, a start-up with a team of scientists discovering techniques in which ultra ultra-capacitors could be used as a fuel in electric and hybrid vehicles. They also seemed favourably favourable as the power supplies for missiles.

Ultra Ultra-capacitors were stronger than batteries and could hold a more reliable charge over long periods of time. Musk began using the capacitors as the base for some of his business strategy tests at Penn University. In the evenings, Musk would go to Rocket Science Games, a start-up founded in Palo Alto that sought to make the most innovative video games ever made by moving them off cassettes and on CDs that could store more data. The CDs would in principle, let them take Hollywood-style storytelling and production excellence to the video games. A team of engineers and film people was brought together to pull off the work. This venture gave Musk a taste of what Silicon Valley had to offer. Musk would turn up around 5 P.M. every evening to write codes. After a short while, he ended up creating what he sought to create. Musk was asked to write the codes that would allow joysticks and mouse connect with numerous computers and games. Musk, a self self-learnt programmer, was vexing to figure out how to multitask things so that one could read video from a CD meanwhile running a game at the same time. He had to give instructions that spoke right to a processor and fidgeted with the rudimentary tasks that made the device function.

(Musk stumbled in Silicon Valley upon riches of opportunities. He graduated with dual degrees from Penn. He primarily envisioned to follow with a Ph.D. in Materials Science and Physics at Stanford and to take forward the work he had completed at Pinnacle on ultra ultra-capacitors. He dropped out of Stanford after two days. He talked his brother into moving to Silicon Valley. The idea for an Internet-based business came to him during his time as an intern. A salesperson tried to sell him the idea of an online listing. This got Musk thinking. In 1995, the brothers created Global Link Information Network, which was eventually renamed as Zip2.

In April 2007, a physicist named John O'Reilly filed a complaint claiming that Musk had lifted the idea for Zip2. According to the complaint, he first met Musk in October 1995. He had started a company named Internet Merchant

Channel, or IMC, which intended to let companies make original, information-packed online ads. Zip2 ended up providing a very similar service. O'Reilly alleged that Musk had first heard about this type of technology while trying to get a job working as a salesman for IMC. The court found that O'Reilly lacked the essential lawful standing to bring this case judge, however, found that O'Reilly lacked the necessary legal standing. The judge ordered O'Reilly to pay $125,000 for Musk's legal fees in 2010.)

The Zip2 idea was original. Few small companies in 1995 understood the Internet and didn't find the value in making a website for their business. Musk and Kimbal wanted to persuade restaurants, clothing shops, and hairdressers etc. to make their existence known to the Web-surfing community. Zip2 would craft a searchable almanack of companies and tie it to maps. The Musk brothers rented a studio-apartment-sized office and bought some rudimentary equipment. It was a three-story building.

To get a fast Internet connection, they drilled a hole in the wall near the Zip2 door and then laced an Ethernet cable down the stairwell to the ISP. Musk did all the coding himself, while Kimbal looked after the door-to-door sales process. They acquired an inexpensive certificate to a catalogue of business listings in the Area. Musk then contacted Navteq, a company that had created digital maps and directions and struck a bargain. They then combined the two databases to get a basic system up. With time, Zip2 brought in more maps to cover regions outside of main urban areas and to build directions. Musk's father gave $28,000 to his sons to help them through. Musk and his brother lived at the office. They had a small closet where they kept their clothes and would shower at the YMCA. Sometimes they ate four meals a day at Jack in the Box.

Zip2 required old-fashioned door-to-door salesmanship. Traders had to be convinced of the Internet's profits. In late 1995, the Musk brothers started hiring their first employs and gathering a sales team. A handful of salespeople joined him and toiled for commissions. Musk did not once leave the office. While Musk did coding, Kimbal became the sales leader. He tried to persuade companies to sign up with Zip2, elucidating that a paid for listing would send a company to the top of search results. But, no one was buying. People said that advertising on the Internet sounded like the dumbest thing they had ever heard of.

The only positive thing happening was the improvements that Musk was making with the Zip2 software. The software had transformed from a proof-of-concept to an actual product that could be used. Moreover, Musk built a huge box around a standard PC and plugged the unit into wheels. When potential financiers would show up, he would roll the massive machine out. It appeared as Zip2 was running inside a mini-supercomputer. Musk told one venture capitalist, "My mentality is that of a samurai. I would rather commit Seppuku than fail." Greg Kouri, a Canadian businessman in his mid-thirties, met Musk in Toronto and bought into the early Zip2 thinking. He gave them a check of $6,000 to start with the business. In 1996, he moved to California and joined Zip2 as a co-founder. Kouri had real business knowledge and expertise at understanding people. He served as the adult supervision at the company. He ended up becoming a mentor.

(Kouri died of a heart attack in 2012 at the age of 51, having made a fortune investing in Musk's companies. Musk attended his funeral).

In 1996, Zip2 experienced a huge transformation. The venture capital firm Mohr Davidow Ventures showed interest in Musk brothers' startup. A meeting was fixed between the brothers and the firm. The brothers pitched the idea to the company well enough and left the investors impressed. Mohr Davidow decided to invest $3 million into the company. With funds in hand, the company's name was changed from Global Link to Zip2. The brothers then moved to a larger office and started employing talented engineers. The company also changed its business strategy. The company had one of the best navigation systems, and they decided to take it from concentrating only on the Bay Area to one having a national scope. Now the company instead of selling its service door-to-door, created software that could be sold to newspapers, which could build directories for real estate, auto dealers, and classifieds. Zip2's software could give newspapers an easy way of getting virtual without having to create their technology from zero. Zip2 now chased bigger clients to get a cut of a countrywide web of listings. This transition of the business model proved to be an influential moment in Musk's life. Musk was pushed into the role of chief technology officer and Rich Sorkin, formerly employed at Creative Labs, a maker of audio equipment, was hired as the company's CEO.

Though Musk had outshone as a self-trained coder, his abilities weren't virtually as refined as those of the fresh appoints. They began reworking the massive bulk of the software. Musk stiffened at some of their alterations, but they could divide the software projects into portions that could be transformed and polished, whereas Musk wrote large chunks of code that could go bonkers for multiple reasons. The engineers also brought with them a more professional working structure and accurate deadlines to the engineering group. This was a welcome change from Musk's overly optimistic deadlines. Starting Zip2 and watching it grow instilled Musk with confidence. He learned to modify his behaviour in certain ways.

For Elon, the word 'no' does not exist. He always set high targets for himself and his team. He continued to be the ball of energy around the office. Before any visit by the investors, Musk would instruct the staff to get on the phone to create a buzzy atmosphere.

With the financiers pouring money, the two brothers spent $30,000 each to buy cars. Kimbal upgraded to a BMW 3 Series, and Musk bought a Jaguar E-Type.

Zip2 had remarkable success. The New York Times, Knight Ridder, Hearst Corporation, and other media properties were its clients. Some of these companies contributed $50 million in additional funding for Zip2. Zip2 attained a brand for its "We Power the Press" motto, and the arrival of money kept it growing fast. In 1997, the company moved into gaudier, more voluminous quarters at 444 Castro Street in Mountain View. It annoyed Musk that the company had turned into a behind-the-scenes player. He strongly believed in the potential of the company to offer fascinating services directly to customers. He bought the domain name city. Com with plans of turning it into a consumer destination. But, Sorkin and the board decided to stick to a conservative path. In April 1998, Zip2 merged with its main competitor City Search in a $300 million deal. The new company would retain the City Search name, while Sorkin would head up the venture. The decision had been announced in the press and seemed inevitable. The merger required the two companies to go over each other's books and to decide which employees would be fired. Musk turned against the deal. In May 1998, the companies cancelled the merger.

Musk urged Zip2's board to oust Sorkin, but instead, he lost his chairmanship. Musk still wanted to go the consumer route but was denied the approval. In February 1999, the PC maker Compaq Computer offered to pay $307 million in cash for Zip2. Company's board accepted the offer. Mohr Davidow made twenty 20 times its original investment, and Musk and Kimbal made $22 million and $15 million, respectively. As soon as the sell-out was over, Elon was on to his next project.

❑

PayPal

The success of his first startup brought immense cash and confidence to Elon. He had become what he always wanted to be, i.e., a dot-com millionaire. His next project would only add to his success story.

After Zip2, Musk was looking for an industry that dealt with cash and inadequacies that he could exploit. He recalled his time at the Bank of Nova Scotia. The biggest take away from that job was that investors are rich and dumb. During his time at the bank, he had been asked to take a look at the company's third-world debt collection.

During his research, he found that countries all through South America and away had failed to pay compelling the bank to write off some of its debt. Musk began to dig into the bank's holdings, and while doing so, he stumbled upon a business opportunity. The government of The United States to reduce the debt burden of developing countries had issued Brady bonds. Through such bonds, the American government backstopped the debt of South American countries. Musk calculated the backstop value. It was 50cents on the dollar, whereas the real debt was trading at 25twenty-five cents. Musk called Goldman Sachs and asked for how much Brazilian debt was available at the 25-cents price. When the person on the other side of the phone confirmed that there were a lot of them, Musk hung up the phone.

He then rushed to pitch the opportunity to his boss. But, the proposal was ultimately rejected. He was told that the bank had burned on Brazilian and Argentinean debt before and didn't want to deal with it again. Later in life, as Elon competed against the banks, he would think back to this moment. He realised that all the investors did to copy what others did. In the later years, Musk deliberated on starting an Internet bank. He was aware of the inevitable transition coming in finance towards online systems. Musk stayed convinced that the finance industry required a major upgrade and that he could have a huge effect on banking with a small investment. Money doesn't require big infrastructure upgrading to do stuff with it. But those were the days when people were hardly at ease buying even books online and exposing their bank accounts to the internet was out of the question. Musk desired to construct a full-service commercial institution online - a company with savings, checking, brokerage, and insurance services. The expertise required to build such a service was available, but the red tape required to cross to create an online bank from zero seemed like an obdurate problem. Impervious to the difficulties, Musk kick-started this new plan even before Zip2 had been sold.

In January 1999, Musk began working on his new plan. He had become a multimillionaire at the age of 27. With his $22 million, he moved into a 1,800-square-foot feet condo. He also bought a $1 million McLaren F1 sports car and a small prop plane that he learned to fly. At that time, there were only 62 McLarens in the world, and he owned one of them. By now, his hair had started thinning. One day, Musk, while driving down the Sand Hill Road to meet with an investor, turned to a friend in the car and said, "Watch this." He stunned the car, spun out, and hit an embankment. This sent the car rotating in mid mid-air like a Frisbee. The windows and wheels were blown away, and the body of the car got severely damaged.

Musk invested the bigger chunk of the money he made from Zip2 into X.COM, an online bank. He invested about $12 million into X.COM and was left with, after taxes, $4 million for personal use. Instead of relying on outside investors, Musk took it upon himself to finance his next venture. He was a rarity in the Silicon Valley, someone who was ready to take huge gambles on himself. He also started to improve his style of entering a complex business and not knowing the industry's nuances bother him.

He believed that the bankers were doing finance all wrong and that he could run the business better than anyone else could. The making of X.COM reflected his creativity, relentless drive, aggressive style, and leadership potentials. He was also to experience for the second time the feeling of being pushed aside by his own company. He gathered an excellent crew to start X.COM. An engineer in his team named Ho had worked at SGI and Zip2, and his colleagues excelled at coding and team-management skills. A pair of Canadian finance specialists—Harris Fricker and Christopher Payne joined them. Musk had met Fricker during his time as an intern at the Bank of Nova Scotia. Fricker brought the understanding of the banking world's workings that X.COM needed. Christopher Payne was Fricker's comrade from the finance community. The four men, Musk, Ho, Harris Fricker, and Christopher

Payne, were the co-founders of the company, while Musk remained the largest shareholder. X.COM started, at a house where the co-founders began thinking, and then moved to proper offices at 394 University Avenue in Palo Alto. They all believed in the idea that the banking sector was running behind the times. Going to a bank's division to speak with a cashier appeared outdated given the fact that the Internet had arrived. The four men were inspired enough to make radical changes in the banking system.

Musk had little experience in the banking sector. Hence, he bought a book on the industry to help him comprehend its inner workings. Moreover, there were a lot of regulatory issues hindering the formation of an online bank. With passing time, the egos began to clash as well. Musk, the superstar in Silicon Valley, had the media drooling over him whereas, for other members of the team, X.COM was their chance to make a mark in the world. Fricker, wanted to run X.COM more conventionally, whereas Musk wanted to rethink the entire banking industry. Elon did not want it to be a regular business milieu and wanted to append normal business thinking.

The dispute between Fricker and Musk came to a foul end. Only five months after X.COM had started, Fricker said that either he took over as CEO or he was going to create his own company. Musk didn't give in to blackmailing. He tried to persuade Ho and other engineers into staying, but they took side with Fricker and left. He was left with only a handful of loyal employees.

Musk was struggling with the funding for X.COM. To raise funds, he went to venture capitalists. Mike Moritz, a famed investor from Sequoia Capital, backed the company. Musk managed to attract engineers from Silicon Valley once again. With every passing week, more and more engineers arrived. The company secured itself a banking license and a mutual fund license and formed a partnership with Barclays. By November, the team had created world's first online banks, with options for insurance, and three mutual funds to choose from. In 1999, X.COM went live to the public. The company tried out some drastic marketing concepts. For example, the customers received a $20 cash card simply by signing up and $10 card for referrals. There were no fees and overdraft penalties. The company also built a person-to-person payment system in which one could send someone money simply by putting their e-mail addresses into the site. The idea was to move away from old styled, slow-moving banks, and to create an active bank account where one could move money around with a couple of clicks. More than 200,000 people bought into it and signed up for X.COM within the first couple of months of operation.

PayPal

Very soon, X.COM had a major opponent. Engineers named Max Levchin, and Peter Thiel had been working on a payment system of their own which they had named Confinity. It soon began offering Web- and e-mail-based payments with their service known as PayPal. The two companies were in a rush to outdo each other's features and attract more users. The rules of the game were simple, whoever got bigger faster would win. Millions of dollars were spent on promotions, while millions were lost battling hackers. To win this race, Musk kept inventing tactics to counter the gain PayPal had established on sale sites like eBay. In March 2000, X.COM and Confinity lastly decided to join forces.

Soon after the deal, X.COM raised $100 million from investors including Deutsche Bank and Goldman Sachs and boasted of more than one million customers. The two companies tried hard to integrate their work cultures. But, like every other merger, disputes began to break out over topics like the design of the company's technology infrastructure and choosing between Linux and Microsoft. Only two months after the merger, Thiel left the company and Levchin threatened to walk out. Musk was again left with a broken team. Moreover, the company began facing a range of new technology issues as the computing systems failed to keep up with an increasing customer base. The company's website collapsed more often. The engineers were asked to design a new system. This diverted key technical staffs and left X.COM susceptible to scam. The company faced multiple frauds. The banks and credit card companies hiked their fees, and the company faced more competition from start-ups. A large number of staff at the company began questioning Musk's decision-making in the face of all the crises. And moreover, at one night, the unexpected happened. A small crowd of X.COM employees met one night and brainstormed over how to push Musk out of the company. They decided to make Thiel the new CEO.

Musk and Justine had got married in January 2000. About 9 months later, in September, they planned to go on a fund-raising trip in Sydney and also catch the Olympics alongside. During their trip, one night, the company's administrators sent letters of no confidence to the company's board. As soon as Elon landed, he found that Thiel had replaced the Musk. He hopped on the next plane back to Palo Alto. For a short-term, he tried to fight back. He insisted the panel to reassess its verdict. But, once it became clear that the company had moved on, Musk yielded. By June 2001, his influence on the company began fading rapidly. That month, Thiel rebranded X.COM as PayPal. However, he embraced his role of advisor to the company and kept investing in it, later becoming company's largest shareholder.

Over next few months, the stock market witnessed a sudden change. The dot-com bubble had burst, and investors wanted to move to cash out in every way possible. One fine morning, the executives at eBay approached PayPal for an acquisition. The majority of the investors wanted to sell fast. Musk, however, advised the board to discard some proposals and hold out for more dough. The company had profits of about $240 million per year, and it seemed like it will go public. Musk's struggle paid off and then in July 2002, eBay offered $1.5 billion for PayPal, and Musk and the rest of the board accepted the contract. Musk made about $250 million from the sale.

❑

The Criticism

The PayPal incident was a mixed bag of ups and lows for Musk. His standing as a forerunner writhed in the aftershock of the deal, and the newspapers turned on him. Eric Jackson, a former Confinity employee, wrote the book -"'The PayPal Wars: Battles with eBay, the Media, the Mafia, and the Rest of Planet Earth" in 2004. In the book, he recalled the company's journey. The book portrayed Musk as an egoist and stubborn person, who was continuously making wrong decisions at every occasion. It also portrayed Thiel and Levchin as prodigies. Valleywag, a gossip website, resorted to bashing Musk in all of its articles. The tone of the book along with the blog's posts incited Musk in 2007 into writing a 2,200-word e-mail to Valleywag. In the email, he gave a real insight to turn of events at PayPal. In it, he also mentioned the seven reasons why he deserved the co-founder status of PayPal. The reason he listed included his part as company's major stockholder, the employing of a lot of the topmost talent, the making of a number of the company's most fruitful business ideas, and his time as CEO when the company went from sixty to several hundred employees.

One of the reasons for Musk going away was that he did not reassure the board on things like the brand change from X.COM to PayPal. Moreover, for the technology change, his decision to stick with Microsoft instead of Linux wasn't well understood. In the 2000s, there were not enough software libraries for Linux that one can find today. Whereas, Microsoft had huge support libraries.

A large number of PayPal's former employees are of the belief that Musk mishandled the branding, technology infrastructure, and fraud situations. Such criticisms brought out the long long-winded counteroffensives from Musk, which reflect his take on events. The stronger critique of Musk was that he was an argumentative know-it-all and his plentiful ego generated profound, lasting breaks within his companies. Though Musk intentionally vexed to temper his conduct, the struggles were not sufficient to win over financiers and other executives. At Zip2 and PayPal, the firms decided that Musk was not yet CEO material. It is also said that Musk oversold his companies' technology.

All this criticism goes against Musk's track record. He always could read people and technology. While others thought of ways to use the Internet's facilities, he had already set off on a focused path. He pioneered many other wonders of technology—directories, maps, sites that focused on vertical markets etc. He made the great leap onward to complete Internet banking. He brought financial instruments online and modernised the industry with a host of new concepts. He exhibited a deep insight into human nature that helped his companies pull off exceptional marketing, technology, and financial feats. Thanks to Musk's guidance, PayPal survived the bursting of the dot-com bubble, became the first smash hit IPO after the 9/11 assaults, and then traded to eBay for a huge sum while the industry was stuck in a theatrical slump. PayPal also became the greatest accumulations of commercial and technical aptitude in Silicon Valley history. The creators of start-ups such as YouTube, Palantir Technologies, and Yelp all worked at PayPal. The PayPal workforce forged methods in combating online fraud that has created the basis of software used by the CIA and FBI to track terrorists and of software used by the world's largest banks to combat crime. By 2014, PayPal had accumulated more than 153 million users and was valued at close to $32 billion as an individual corporation. After its success, floods of payment and banking start-ups have popped up all over. Although Musk's goals can sound ridiculous at the moment, he surely trusts in them and, when given sufficient time, he surely achieves them.

Musk and Justine, like any couple, had their ups and downs. The two, for some time, scuffled for a few days about phone calls that Justine kept getting from an ex-boyfriend. Elon and Justine had a major fight. A few minutes later, when Musk cooled down, he went down on his knees to propose her for marriage. Justine, as Musk had expected, yielded to the proposal.

At their wedding reception, Musk pulled her close while they danced, and informed her that she was the alpha in that relationship. Only two months later, Justine signed a post-nuptial financial contract and moved into a long drawn battle. The coup at X.COM did not facilitate the situation. They had to postpone their honeymoon because of it. Only in late December in 2000, the things began to calm down. Now was when Musk took his first vacation in years. It was a two-week trip, starting with Brazil and then South Africa. In Africa, Musk contracted malaria. He was bedridden for a few days. He spent ten days in the intensive care unit.

❑

The Space Odyssey

•

On his 30th birthday in June 2001, Musk realised that X.COM, the company that he founded, had been ripped away from him and given to someone else to run. The life around start-ups had become utterly monotonous, and so had the Silicon Valley—the hub of start-ups. It had become a big a trade show where everybody worked in the tech industry and talked all the time of funding, IPOs, and racing for big payouts. The idea of absconding this very rewarding rat race began to become more and more attractive to him. He had spent his whole life chasing a bigger stage, and Palo Alto was like a stepping-stone en route the destination. Elon and Justine moved to Los Angeles and began the next chapter of their lives. Apart from the city's glitz and grandeur, what else attracted Musk was the space that it offered. After the PayPal episode, Musk started revisiting his childhood imaginations that revolved around rocket ships and space travel. He began to think that he might have a better calling than building Internet facilities.

Musk's move to Los Angeles was out of his lust for the access to space or at least the space industry that the city offered. It is an ideal city for the aeronautics industry. The U.S. Air Force, NASA, Boeing, and many other organisations carry out their manufacturing and experimentation in and around L.A. (Los Angeles). The city is a major hub for the military's aeronautics work and commercial activity. Though Musk didn't know precisely what he sought to do in space, he understood that simply by being in L.A. he would be encircled by the world's best aeronautics sages. Their company could aid him to improve his ideas, and moreover, in L.A., there would be no dearth of recruits to join his ensuing project. His first exchanges with the aeronautics community were with a group of space enthusiasts. They were participants of a non-profit group called the Mars Society, a group dedicated to exploring and settling on the Red Planet. It planned to organise a fund-raising campaign in mid-2001. The event took place at the house of one of the Mars Society members. Robert Zubrin, the head of the group, was left stunned by the rejoinder sent by Musk, whom no one had invited. He signed a check for five thousand dollars to the community. This made everybody take notice. Zubrin invited him for coffee. Over the coffee, he began to amuse Musk with stories of the research center the society had built in the Arctic to simulate the harsh environment of Mars and the tests they had been running for something called the Trans life Mission, in which there would be a rotating case circling Earth that was directed by a team of mice. This spin gave them one-third gravity—the same that exists on Mars. At the event's dinner, Musk met the director and space buff James Cameron, and Carol Stoker, a planetary expert from NASA who had a profound interest in Mars. During the dinner, he came across the model for an aircraft that would fly over Mars looking for water. Musk loved the idea. He joined the board of directors of 'Mars Society' and signed another check of $100,000, which would fund a research station in the desert.

By now, Musk had truly started thinking about investing in the technologies of the future. He wanted to do something with the solar power. He wanted to do something bigger than the Mars Society. Instead of sending a few mice into the Earth's orbit, he wanted to send them to Mars. The journey's estimates were set at $15 million. The more he thought about space; the more important its exploration seemed to him. He was of the opinion that the public had lost some of its motivation and faith for the future. Musk had begun to think about the space travel in a very serious manner. He desired to motivate the masses and revive their hunger for science. His doubts that men folk had lost its will to push the boundaries were proven correct when he accessed the NASA website. He was taken aback by the lack of any plan for Mars exploration on the website. It was time for him to take matters into his own hands.

The journey to Mars began in a hotel conference room. Musk assembled his network of contacts in the space industry at a series of hotels. He wanted them to help him develop the mice-to-Mars idea or at least to come up with something similar. Musk expected to capture the world's attention, and get people thinking about Mars. The experts at the meetings had to figure out a demonstration that would be feasible at a price tag of about $20 million. Musk resigned from the Mars Society and announced his organisation—the Life to Mars Foundation. It had a huge collection of talent. Scientists from NASA formed a large part of this pool of talent. The foundation's events were attended by James Cameron and Michael Griffin, whose academic credentials included degrees in aerospace engineering, electrical engineering, civil engineering, and applied physics. Griffin had worked for the CIA's venture capital arm called In-Q-Tel, and also had been a former employee at Orbital Sciences Corporation, a maker of satellites and spacecraft. Griffin was working for Musk as space thinker- in- chief. The experts were thrilled and happily debated the qualities and possibility of sending rodents in space. During the discussions, a consensus began taking shape around following a different project called Mars Oasis. This plan required Musk to buy a rocket and use it to shoot a robotic greenhouse towards Mars. A team of scientists had already started working on a space-ready growth chamber for plants. The plan was to revise their structure to sow it in the Martian soil. This, in turn, would produce the first oxygen on Mars. The idea seemed both flashy and feasible.

Musk coveted that it must have a window and a means to direct an audiovisual response to Earth. This would have allowed people to watch the plant grow. There were plans of sending out sets to students around the country who could grow their plants at the same time and take notice of facts like the Martian plant could grow twice as high as its Earth-bound counterpart in the same amount of time. Musk's interest in the idea began to inspire the space groups across the world, many of whom had gone pessimistic about anything fresh happening in space again. The main thing upsetting about the whole plan was the budget. Musk had decided upon a budget of $20 million-–$30 million for the project. But by the industry's parameters that was only enough to cover the cost of a rocket launch alone. Besides, there were huge manufacturing challenges that needed to be solved first. For example, putting up a window was a serious thermal problem. Also, it was not possible to keep the container warm enough to keep anything alive. Lifting Martian soil seemed like a bad idea as it might be toxic. The idea of growing the plant in a nutrient-rich gel instead was also discussed, but Musk insisted that it would weaken the whole point of the attempt. Some scientists invented a variety of very resilient mustard seeds which that could survive the Martian soil. Musk turned some of the volunteer thinkers into advisors and put them to work on the plant machine's plan. He then planned a trip to Russia to find out exactly how much a launch could cost. He wanted to buy a renovated intercontinental ballistic missile, or ICBM, from the Russians and use that as his launch vehicle.

Musk contacted Jim Cantrell. Cantrell had done some classified and unclassified work for the United States and other governments. He had also been accused of espionage and placed under house arrest in 1996 by the Russians. In late October 2001, Musk, Cantrell, and Adeo Ressi, Musk's friend from college, boarded a flight to Moscow. Team Musk later went on to include Mike Griffin and met with the Russians three times over a period of next four months.

Musk had a budget of $20 million. When he asked Russians how much a missile would cost, the reply was $8 million each. Musk countered. He said "$8 million for two". The Russians did not take him seriously and thought he did not have money enough to cement the deal.

By the end of February 2002, Musk and his team had been unable to ink any deal with the Russians. Musk had come to Russia complete with the hope of saving humanity but was now returning infuriated and dissatisfied. Only the Russians had the rockets that could fit within his budget. Now he had only one option left, to make it himself.

Musk had a plan in his mind. He had done the calculations that would have allowed to undercut the costs. He wished to build a modest-sized rocket that would cater to a part of the market that was dedicated to transporting smaller satellites and research payloads to space. He had also thought out the theoretical performance features of the rocket. He had spent months learning and observing the aerospace industry and the physics behind it. He borrowed texts like Rocket Propulsion Elements, Fundamentals of Astrodynamics, and Aerothermodynamics of Gas Turbine and Rocket Propulsion. Musk had returned to his juvenile state as a seeker of knowledge and had appeared from this contemplative procedure with the understanding that rockets can and must be made much inexpensive than what the Russians were proposing. Forget the mice or plant; Musk had decided to motivate people to contemplate travelling in space by making the space exploration cheaper.

As people in the space industry came to know of Musk's plans, noises were made, apprehensions were raised. One of the harbingers of Musk's plan was Tom Muller.

❑

Tom Muller

•

Tom was the son of a logger based in the town of St. Marries. He was always different from the kids of his age. While the rest of the kids ventured into the woods during winter, he stayed in the library, busy reading books. During his childhood years, Mueller grew an interest in machines. He once repaired a broken clock and turned it into a school project. He also repaired the family's lawn mower when it stopped working out of blue. Later in his life, Mueller got interested in rockets. He bought kits, which that had instructions on building small rockets.

Very soon, he graduated to building his rockets. At the tender age of twelve, he shaped a model space shuttle. A couple of years later, he borrowed his dad's welding gear to make a rocket engine prototype. The prototype won a couple of science competitions.

Mueller ultimately settled down at mechanical engineering. After finishing college, he worked with Hughes Aircraft on satellites and then with TRW Space & Electronics where he conducted tests with propellants and also supervised the development of the firm's TR-106 engine, a huge machine powered by liquid oxygen and hydrogen. He was also a part of the Reaction Research Society, a group formed in 1943 to support the construction of rockets. His biggest achievement was an 80-pound machine that could yield 13,000 pounds of thrust, which was also the world's largest liquid-fuel rocket engine at the time.

In January 2002, at the workshop of John Garvey, a former employee at the aerospace company McDonnell Douglas, the two men were working on an 80-pound engine when Garvey brought up Musk's name. On a Sunday morning, Musk paid a visit to the garage.

Mueller and Musk talked for hours. Musk instantly understood that he had found someone he could rely upon. Later on, Musk introduced him to his team of space experts. Mueller worked on the performance and the cost metrics of the rocket. The rocket was not to carry large-sized satellites, but instead was aimed at the lower end of the satellite market, and was poised to become an ideal for an emerging class of smaller payloads. The success of the rocket could open new markets for both commercial and research payloads. Musk wanted to be at the forefront of this ushering into a new era in space.

PayPal's shares rose drastically by 55 percent. This increased Musk's net worth to hundreds of millions. In the April of 2002, Musk completely abandoned the idea for publicity and instead committed all his efforts towards building a commercial space venture.

❑

The Advent In Space

In June 2002, Musk's new venture Space Exploration Technologies, or as famously called SpaceX, came to life. It was set in an old warehouse at 1310 East Grand Avenue in El Segundo, at the outskirts of Los Angeles. The surroundings of the warehouse were sparse, with a dusty floor and a forty feet high ceiling with wooden beams and lining which curved at the top to give the place a hangar-like feel. In the north side of the edifice was an office space with compartments and rooms. During the first week of its operations, SpaceX's building was filled with delivery trucks carrying Dell laptops and printers and folding tables.

Musk transformed the SpaceX office by applying a glossy coating over the concrete on the floors, and a fresh coat of white paint on the walls. The desks were spread across the building. This ensured that computer scientists and engineers could sit with the welders building the hardware. This unorthodox approach of SpaceX proved beneficial for the company in the long run.

The company's mission was set to emerge as the "Southwest Airlines of Space." SpaceX would build its engines and outsource the manufacturing of the other components of the rocket. It gained an edge over the other companies in the market by building a better, cheaper engine, and by fine-tuning the assembly process. This helped it make rockets faster and cheaper than any other company in the market. The process included the production of a type of mobile launch vehicle that could travel to various sites, take the rocket from a horizontal to vertical position, and send it off to space. The company aimed to develop such expertise in this process that it could make multiple rockets launches a month, earn money from each such launches, and ultimately eliminate the need to rely on government funds.

SpaceX was about to revolutionise the rocket business, which Musk felt had not changed in about fifty 50 years. The companies faced little or no competition at all, and hence they used to manufacture extremely expensive machines that failed to achieve maximum performance. Musk brought a revolutionary change in the production. He began applying some of the start-up techniques he had learnt in the Silicon Valley. His style of administration allowed SpaceX to capitalise on the huge improvements in the computers that had taken place over the past decade. SpaceX had also planned to avoid the waste and cost ravages linked with government service providers. SpaceX's first rocket was named Falcon 1. It was an ode to Star Wars' Millennium Falcon. The company promised to send a 1,400-pound payload for $6.9 million on aboard Falcon 1.

By all considerations, it was an ambitious goal to achieve. The deadline for the completion of the first engine was set to be May 2003. The second engine was slated to be completed in June, the body in July, and everything was to be assembled in August. The Launchpad was planned to be constructed in September, and the first launch was to take place in November 2003. The company went to the extent of planning a trip to Mars by the end of the decade.

The company's plans had already found keen observers among the members of the military who had been lobbying for the idea of giving the armed forces better space capabilities. In future, if a conflict breaks out in space, the military wanted the ability to respond with the technology employed for that mission. It was a drastic shift from a system where it used to take more than ten years to build and position a satellite for a specific job. The military wanted inexpensive, smaller satellites that could be reconfigured using the software.

Apart from the military, some companies in the medical and consumer goods industries also showed interest in space technology to study the effects of lack of gravity on their products. But despite the craze that Musk's idea of a cheap rocket launch had created, the odds were not in his favour. The history was rife with examples of U.S. and Soviet rocket launch disasters. From 1957 to 1966, the United States tried to send around 400 rockets into the earth's orbit, and more than 100 of those rockets crashed. SpaceX had the opportunity of being able to learn from the past. The fact that it employed the former staff of companies like Boeing and TRW worked in its favour. But the biggest setback for the company's plans was the lack of budget that could not support a string of explosions. SpaceX only had three or four attempts at making the Falcon 1 work.

The $1.5 billion that Musk made by selling his stakes in Pay Pal gave him some liquidity and added more than $100 million to his wealth. Musk invested this money in SpaceX. This ensured that no one in future would be able to take control of SpaceX away from Musk unlike before.

Amidst all this action, Justine gave birth to a son, who was later named Nevada Alexander Musk. Nevada was only ten weeks old when he died of sudden infant death syndrome. The child spent three days on life support in a hospital in Orange County before his life support was withdrawn.

After Nevada's death, Musk began spending more and more of his time at SpaceX. He went on to hire the top talent for the company. Apart from Mueller, he went on to hire Chris Thompson, a one- time marine who had managed the production of the Delta and Titan rockets at Boeing. Thompson joined the company as the vice president of operations. Also, Tim Buzza, known as one of the world's leading rocket testers became a part of the team. The early days also witnessed the arrival of Mary Beth Brown, one of Musk's most trusted employees. Over the years, she brought Musk meals, set up his business appointments, arranged a time with his children, picked out his clothes, dealing with press requests, and when required pulled Musk out of meetings to keep him on schedule.

The engineers at SpaceX were young, male overachievers. Elon would himself go to the aerospace departments of the country's top colleges and inquire there about the best performers. He very often called the students in their hostel rooms and recruited them over the phone. Most of the times, the students used to take his call for a prank call and looked Musk up on the Internet after hanging up. These young aeronautics geniuses found an exciting opportunity in Musk's offer. It was one of those rare opportunities where it did not require them to join a bureaucratic government contractor.

SpaceX first project was the construction of a gas generator that produces hot gas. A team of engineers assembled it in Los Angeles and then put it into the back of a pickup truck and drove it out to Mojave, California, to test it. The first ignition run took place at 11 A.M. It lasted ninety 90 seconds. Though the generator worked well, it let out a black smoke cloud. The results of this test were far from perfect. In the days that followed, SpaceX's team carried out multiple tests a day and ultimately had the gas generator tuned to their needs after two weeks of work.

Jeremy Hollman was one of the first engineers to work with SpaceX. He had studied aerospace engineering at Iowa State University and had also completed masters in aerospace engineering from the University of Southern

California. He had also spent years working as a test engineer at Boeing. The time at Boeing had left him unimpressed as he found the nature of the work to be unchallenging. So, when Musk came along with his offer, Hollman spent no time accepting it. Hollman later went on to become Mueller's second in command.

Mueller developed a 3D computer model of the two jet engines he wanted to build. The engine for the first stage of the Falcon 1 was named Merlin. Its job was to lift it off the ground. The second stage engine was named Kestrel. It was to power the upper, second stage of the rocket and guide it in space. Together, Hollman and Mueller figured out which parts of the engines were to be built at the factory and which parts were to be bought. During the trials, Hollman found changing the seals on car wash valves made them compatible to be used with rocket fuel.

As soon as SpaceX completed its first engine at the factory in California, Hollman put it into a trailer and drove it to Texas at the test site. A group led by Mueller began exploring the intricacies of the engines. While the navy and Beal had left some testing apparatus, SpaceX had to build a large amount of custom gear. One of the largest of these structures was a horizontal test stand about 30 feet long, 15 feet wide, and 15 feet tall. Moreover, both the engines Kestrel and Merlin came with challenges. Mueller looked at the test data to spot places where the engine ran hot or cold or had a flaw. After spotting a flaw, he would call California and engineers there would alter the parts and send them off to Texas. To get to space, the Merlin engine would need to burn for 180 seconds whereas it would burn for only a half second before it stopped. Many times it vibrated too much during the tests, or responded badly to new material, or cracked and needed major part upgrades, like moving from an aluminium manifold to a manifold made out of the more exotic In conel, an alloy suited to extreme temperatures. Once a fuel valve did not open properly and caused the whole engine to blow up.

Sometimes Musk too took part in the testing process. One such time was when the SpaceX's engineers were trying to perfect a cooling chamber for its engines. During the initial test, one such cooling chamber cracked. During the second test, another one broke too. Musk insisted on conducting a third test too. Now this time the third chamber cracked too. Musk wasted no time and flew the hardware back to California. There he, with the help of some engineers, started to fill the chambers with epoxy to see if it could seal them. The tests yield no positive results, and hence he asked his engineers to come up with a new solution.

SpaceX had developed the feeling of a small, tight-knit family. Everyone worked as a part of one big team. Very soon the company earned a customer as well. Its first rocket was to launch in early 2004 from Vandenberg Air Force Base, carrying a satellite called TacSat-1 for the Department of Defence. Now with such a mammoth- sized goal looming, 12-hour days, six days a week became the norm at SpaceX. Musk decided to unveil a prototype of Falcon 1 to the public in December 2003. He had planned for a press conference and an event in Washington that would tell the world that a modern, smarter, cheaper rocket maker had arrived.

The event was well received. A few weeks later, SpaceX made an astonishing announcement. SpaceX revealed plans for a second rocket. Along with the Falcon 1, it would build the Falcon 5. This rocket was to have five engines and could carry about 9,200 pounds. Falcon 5 could also reach the International Space Station (ISS) for resupply missions. This capability allowed SpaceX to bid for NASA contracts. And setting new parameters of safety, the rocket could complete its missions even if three of the five engines failed.

Musk was always looking for brainy engineers who apart from having done well at school have also done something exceptional with their talents. Whenever he finds the right fit, he asks him or her to come to SpaceX. As the recruits began to arrive, SpaceX acquired several other buildings in the El Segundo complex. The employees needed high-speed connections between all the buildings. But SpaceX's neighbouring buildings were blocking its plan to connect all of its buildings via fiber optic lines. Company's IT chief Branden Spikes came up with a plan to squeeze a networking cable safely between the electrical cable, and phone wires on a telephone pole.

Musk's quest to find contractors often ended at suppliers with similar experience from different fields. When SpaceX needed someone to build the fuel tanks, Musk outsourced the work to companies that had made large, metal agricultural tanks used in the dairy and food processing businesses. These suppliers also struggled to keep up with SpaceX's schedule.

The employees at SpaceX were thrilled to be part of the adventure and always pushed their limits to not to let Musk down. But there were some moments where Musk went too far. Engineers felt like Musk's ego had trumped him as he was selling SpaceX as the vanquisher of the aerospace industry when in reality the company was yet to launch successfully. Engineers who pointed out the flaws in the Falcon 5 design or suggested to get the Falcon 1 out quickly were often ignored.

In early 2004, SpaceX hoped to launch its rocket. The Merlin engine was one of the most efficient rocket engines ever made. But it was not until the fall of 2004 that the engines began to burn consistently and meet all the requirements. This meant that the D Day was to arrive soon. This gave the employees at SpaceX jitters as lots of problems abounded the launch. The avionics had stopped working, getting a flash storage drive failed, software needed to manage the rocket also functioned erratically. The process dragged on for six more months. Lastly, in May 2005, SpaceX sent the rocket 180 miles north to Vandenberg Air Force Base for a test fire and completed a five-second burn on the Launchpad.

Launching from Vandenberg gave SpaceX choice of several Launchpads to choose from. SpaceX, though, was told that it would have to wait months to launch. The company began searching for a new site. It had to be a place where the planet spun faster and hence gave rockets an added boost. The first name that came up was Kwajalein Island, the largest island in an atoll between Guam and Hawaii in the Pacific Ocean and part of the Republic of the Marshall Islands. It was the same spot that the U.S. Army had used for decades as a missile test site. In no time they got the permission to fly from the islands. In June 2005, the company began to transport its equipment to the new location.

To reach the Kwaj islands, the employees either flew in Musk's jet or took commercial flights through Hawaii. The only available accommodations were two-bedroom dorms with military-issued dressers and desks. All the materials that were of the need to the engineers had to be flown in or brought by boat from Hawaii. Every morning, the crew gathered their gear and spent forty-five45- minutes on a boat ride to their Launchpad.

The day for the team started at 7 A.M. in the mornings, a series of meetings would take place with people keeping a tab of what needed to get done and debating. The workers would spend hours melding together parts of the rocket. The engineers were continually puzzled by what Musk would trust and what he wouldn't. Someone's demand for buying a $200,000 machine, believed to be vital to Falcon 1's success, would be put down. Whereas he would not hesitate to pay a similar amount to put a shiny surface on the factory floor to make it look nice.

The situation was preposterous. A rookie rocket company was trying to carry out one of the most difficult tasks known to man. Very often the rocket was sent to the Launchpad and raised vertically for days, but meanwhile, the technical and safety checks revealed a host of new problems. In November 2005, the team felt ready to give launching a shot. Musk flew in with his brother, Kimbal.

November 26 was to be the launch day. That day the crew woke up at 3 A.M. to fill the rocket with liquid oxygen. Meanwhile, another team monitored the launch from a control room. Hours before the launch a major problem was detected. A valve on a liquid oxygen tank would not close. The mission had to be aborted. SpaceX began preparing for another attempt in mid-December. It had to be aborted too due to high winds and faulty valves. SpaceX discovered that the rocket's power distribution systems were malfunctioning and would need new capacitors. SpaceX employees flew to get some fresh capacitors. In under eighty 80 hours, the electronics were returned in working order and installed in the rocket.

At last, on March 24, 2006, the rocket was set for launch. The Falcon 1 stood on Launchpad and ignited. Seconds later it went soaring into the sky. Musk watched the action unfold from the control room. Then, about 25 seconds later things went down the hill. A fire broke out above the engine, and it started to spin and tumble back to Earth. The rocket fell onto the launch site. The debris sunk into a reef situated 250 feet from the Launchpad.

Musk and other SpaceX executives blamed the crash on an unnamed technician who apparently had failed to properly tighten a fitting on a fuel pipe, which caused the fitting—an aluminium b-nut to crack. The technician in question was Hollman. After the rocket crash, he flew to Los Angeles in the mood to confront Musk. Hollman knew that he'd fastened the b-nut correctly. After all the debris was analysed, it turned out that the b-nut had cracked due to corrosion from the months in Kwaj's salty atmosphere.

Almost a year after the crash, Musk and the team was ready to go for another launch. The test fire conducted on March 15, 2007, was a successful one. Then, on March 21, Falcon 1 finally surged up and toward space. The first couple of minutes of flight gave reports that the systems were in good shape. After three minutes of flight, the initial stage of the rocket separated and fell back on Earth. Now it was the turn of the Kestrel engine to carry the second stage into orbit. Functioning as per the expectations, the rocket separated as planned. For more than five minutes everything went right. The camera installed on the rocket showed Earth getting smaller and smaller as it made its way into space. But then happened the dreaded. Mueller noticed a tremor that soon turned into a flailing, and the rocket started to break apart and then finally blew up in the sky, scattering its debris in the ocean. The SpaceX engineers wasted no time in figuring out what went wrong. The propellant when consumed, started to move around the tank and slosh against the sides. It sloshed enough to leave an opening to the engine uncovered. When the engine got in contact with air, it flamed out.

This failed test came as a blow to SpaceX's engineers, many of whom had spent two years working on it. The date for the next launch was set about four years after the original target. Moreover, all these failed attempts were taking a toll on Musk's fortune. The math showed that SpaceX could only afford one or two more attempts. But Musk rarely let it show to employees. The failures could do little to curtail his vision.

❑

Electric Elon

•

J.B. Straubel, a science enthusiast since his childhood, was born in Wisconsin. At the young age of 13, Straubel found an old golf cart at the dump, which he restored to working condition. In the late 1890s, Straubel's great-grandfather started the Straubel Machine Company. The company went on to build one of the first internal combustion engines in the United States. The engine was used to power boats. Straubel completed his higher studies at the Stanford University. There he enrolled in 1994 planning to become a physicist. Later, he decided to opt out of physics. He found the subject too theoretical. He developed his own major called energy systems and engineering. It was the time when companies had begun dabbling with new uses for solar power and electric vehicles. Straubel went on to look for these start-ups. He started working on a project of his own in his garage. He bought an old Porsche for $1,600 and turned it into an electric car. The car went on to set the world record for electric vehicle acceleration, travelling a quarter mile in 17.28 seconds.

By 2002, Straubel obtained his master's degree from Stanford and began looking for something that called out to his heart. He finally decided on Rosen Motors. The company had built the world's first hybrid vehicles. They had built a car that ran off a flywheel and a gas turbine and had electric motors to drive the wheel. After finishing his stint at Rosen Motors, Straubel went on to work with Harold Rosen, an engineer known for having invented the geostationary satellite. To make ends meet, he also worked during the nights and on the weekends too. One day, some of his old friends from the Stanford solar car team came to visit him. He came to know that a group of engineers at Stanford were working on solar cars for years. But unfortunately, the university was trying to shut down this group. The group had already competed in some cross-country solar-powered car races. At this point, Straubel got in touch with this group of engineers. He offered them a place to stay. During their stay at Straubel's, the team kept discussing one topic—lithium-ion batteries. They were of the belief that the batteries had improved much more than people realised. Many consumer electronics devices like laptops were running on lithium-ion batteries, which could be strung together. They thought of the possibility of putting ten thousand of the battery cells together.

Now, Straubel began following the solar car crew. He was always developing plans for building an electric car based on the lithium-ion batteries. The design of the car Straubel came up with was a super-aerodynamic vehicle with 80 percent of its mass consisting of the batteries. The plan was less about forming a car company and more about building a proof-of-concept vehicle.

The students at Stanford agreed to join Straubel on the condition if he could raise some money. He began hunting for funds by going to trade shows. He faced several rejections at the hands of the investors before he met Musk in the fall of 2003.

Lunch was set up at a seafood restaurant near the SpaceX headquarters in Los Angeles. When Straubel announced his electric car project, the idea struck an immediate chord with Musk. He promised Straubel $10,000.

After the meeting with Musk, Straubel reached out to his friends at AC Propulsion—- the Los Angeles- based company started in 1992. It specialised in the development of electric vehicles, building passenger to sports cars. Straubel wanted to show Musk his kit car that he had named tzero. It had a fibreglass body on top of a steel frame and could go from zero to 60 miles per hour in 4.9 seconds. Straubel asked the AC Propulsion crew to bring a tzero over for Musk to drive. Musk saw its potential as a fast machine that could change the perception of electric cars. For some months, Musk went on to fund the transformation of the kit car into a commercial vehicle.

At the same time, a couple of other business groups in Northern California had also started working on the idea of making a lithium-ion battery powered car. NuvoMedia, a company created by Martin Eberhard and Marc Tarpenning in 1997 had created one of the first electronic book readers, called the Rocket eBook. The work they did at NuvoMedia gave them great insight into the world of consumer electronics and the remarkably improved lithium-ion batteries. While their invention Rocket eBook was far ahead of its time, it was groundbreaking enough to appeal to Gemstar International Group. Gemstar paid $187 million to acquire the company NuvoMedia.

Martin Eberhard was a talented engineer. The conflicts in the Middle East worried him, and he had started to accept global warming as a reality. He began looking for substitutes for petrol and diesel run cars. He started investigating the potential of hydrogen fuel cells but later found them to be incompetent for the job. Bernhard's interest began to grow in the all-electric cars designed by AC Propulsion. Eberhard went to Los Angeles to convince AC Propulsion into being a commercial enterprise rather than a hobby shop. When they rejected his proposals, Eberhard decided to form his own company and explore the potential of lithium-ion batteries. He began by building a model of the electric car on a spreadsheet. It allowed him to change various components and notice their effects on the vehicle's shape and performance. It allowed him to adjust the weight, some batteries, the resistance of the tires and body, etc. The technology is available at the time allowed for the development of a lighter-weight, high-end sports car. This car was to be fast, fun to drive, and have better range than what people expected.

On July 1, 2003, the duo Eberhard and Tarpenning started their new company. Eberhard had come up with the name Tesla Motors, which was a homage to the inventor Nikola Tesla. The two rented an office with three desks and two small rooms in a building located at 845 Oak

Grove Avenue in Menlo Park. The team soon figured that Nikola Tesla had built an electric motor a century earlier. The tough part of the task at hand was building the factory. But soon they realised that the big automakers don't build their cars anymore.

The Tesla team decided to license technology from AC Propulsion and to use the sleek, ground-hugging Lotus Elise chassis for the body of their car. The team decided to avoid selling their cars through partners and instead sell them directly. The team then went hunting for venture capitalists in January 2004. The company needed an upfront investment of $7 million to make a prototype vehicle. That would give them something physical to show off.

Eberhard and Tar penning expected Musk to back their plan. They were under the impression that he thought differently and would be open to the idea of an electric car. Their expectations came to reality when Tom Gage from AC Propulsion called Eberhard and told him that Musk was looking to fund something in the electric car arena. A meeting with Musk was fixed immediately. Following the meeting, Musk decided to back the project. With an investment of $6.5 million, Musk became the largest shareholder of Tesla and the chairman of the company.

Musk called Straubel and asked him to meet with the Tesla team. Straubel stopped by the office for a meeting and was hired right away at a salary of $95,000 per year. Straubel informed his team of engineers at Stanford about Tesla. Many of them immediately decided to become a part of the company. Tesla now needed to expand to accommodate its growing team and to create a workshop. They located a two-story industrial building in San Carlos at 1050 Commercial Street. The 10,000-square-foot feet space allowed them to build a research and development shop. The left part of the building was made into an office space. The employees painted the office white, made a field trip to IKEA to buy desks, and made an online order of computers.

The plan for making a prototype was to take the AC Propulsion tzero powertrain and fit it into the Lotus Elise body. The company decided to outsource other parts from Asia. The team of engineers at Tesla mainly needed to focus on developing the battery pack systems, wiring the car, and cutting and welding metal. The engineers purchased some machine tools, hand tools, and floodlights and turned the facility into an R&D hub. They studied the Lotus's software to understand how it tied together the pedals, mechanical apparatus, and the dashboard gauges. The real task was to work with the battery pack design. No one before had tried to join hundreds of lithium-ion batteries in parallel. The task before the team was to understand how heat would dissipate and current flow would behave. Then the engineers would test various types of air and liquid cooling mechanisms. The construction began on October 18, 2004, and, four months later, on January 27, 2005, an entirely new kind of car had been built by eighteen 18 people. Musk put in $9 million more as Tesla raised a $13 million.

A few months later, the engineers realised that there was a massive potential flaw in their electric vehicle. When the batteries caught on fire, they went up like a cluster of bottle rockets with close to 7,000 pieces. The possible scale of explosion horrified the engineers. Tesla formed a six-person team to deal with the issue. Tesla moved its explosion research to a blast area. The engineers learned about the inner workings of the batteries. They then worked on developing methods for arranging them in ways that would prevent fires spreading. The success at building two prototype cars boosted the company's confidence.

But before the car could be put to production, there were many more technical and non-technical overhauls that needed to be undertaken. For example, the body of the car had serious issues in both form and function. The door was a foot tall and also the body needed to be longer to accommodate Tesla's battery pack and a trunk. Tesla preferred to construct the car using carbon fiber instead of fibreglass. The company took services of a handful of designers to design the car. A British company, with the help of the digital file, created a plastic version of the car for aerodynamics testing. In May 2006, the company, which had now grown to a hundred employees, built a black version of the car, which was named as EP1. It allowed the company to show investors the growth that had been made and to ask for more funds. The investors were now starting to grasp Tesla's long-term potential. Musk once again put $12 million into Tesla.

In July 2006, Tesla decided to go public about all the developments it had made. The company's prototypes went on display at an event in Santa Monica. Journalists in large numbers attended the event. Celebrities like Arnold Schwarzenegger and former Disney CEO Michael Eisner showed up at the event. The company revealed that each car would cost $90,000 and would have a range of 250 miles per charge. About thirty 30 people committed to buying the cars. The list included technology billionaires like Google co-founders Brin and Page. At the event, Musk promised a cheaper car—a four-seater, four-door model under $50,000, to be launched in about three years.

The car generated a lot of buzz in the automotive world. The appearance of a good-looking, fast electric car stoked everyone's passions. Few months after the Santa Monica event, the Pebble Beach Concours d'Elegance, a famous showcase for exotic cars, was to take place. The organisers of the event begged to have a Tesla at the event and even went to the extent of waiving off the display fees. Tesla's booth at the event witnessed large attendance with people writing $100,000 checks to pre-order their cars. Some even went to the extent of showing up at the Tesla office to buy a car.

Tesla had some trends working in its favour. Advances in computing made it possible for small car companies to punch at the same weight as the giants of the industry. The third prototype went to the same collision testing facility used by large automakers. This gave Tesla access to top-of-the-line high-speed cameras and other imaging technology. Other tests were done by a company that specialised in computer simulations. This saved Tesla from having to build a fleet of crash vehicles. The company also had access to tracks made of cobblestones and concrete entrenched with metal substances. This facility could easily reproduce 100,000 miles and ten years of wear.

Tesla's interactions with Detroit were a reminder of how the great city had isolated itself from its own can-do culture. The company tried to lease a small office in the city, but the city's red tape made it an affliction. What separated Tesla from other companies was its ability to make quick, crisp decisions. Never did it ever get hung up overanalysing a situation. The company would pick a plan of attack, and when it failed at something, it failed fast and then tried a new approach.

Musk wanted the car to be more comfortable. He made the carbon-fiber body a priority, and he pushed for electronic sensors on the doors so that it could be unlocked with the touch of a finger. By 2007, Tesla employed 260 employees. With having produced the fastest, most beautiful electric car, it was rapidly climbing the ladders of success. The next step for it was to go for mass production if of its cars.

The battery supply chain was adding cost and delays to the production. The body panels had to be made in France, while the motors in Taiwan. The battery cells were bought in China and shipped to Thailand. Tesla wanted Lotus to build the body of the car. This meant that Tesla had no chance of turning profits until six to nine months had passed. Musk was concerned about the way company's finances were being managed.

Tesla had managed to keep its employee costs down by hiring the fresh out of Stanford students rather than the proven guys. But in the name of equipment and materials, the company was spending quite a fortune. Musk was confident that the price of the car would come down significantly over time once it improved its manufacturing process and increased its sales. But unfortunately, Musk was wrong about the figures as the production cost of the car was too high to churn any profit.

Company's CEO Eberhard had turned Tesla into a cult of engineering, but in the process, the other parts of the company had been neglected. The high cost of production and the ineffective suppliers were crippling Tesla. Eberhard and Musk had clashed for years over some of the design on the car, but the two shared the same visions for the battery technology and what it could do to the world. But Musk had to do the inevitable. Musk told Eberhard that he would be replaced as CEO.

In August 2007, Eberhard was demoted and named the president of technology. A few months later Eberhard left the company. Soon the problems began mounting for Tesla. The carbon-fiber body turned out to be a huge pain to paint. There were faults in the battery pack and the motor short-circuited time and again. Moreover, the body panels began developing gaps. The engineers had to redesign the car and also shave off some weight.

After removal of Eberhard from the post of CEO, Michael Marks was named as the interim chief. But soon enough Marks's vision for the company began to deviate from that of Musk. On December 3, 2007, Ze'ev Drori replaced Marks as CEO. He was more of an executor of Musk's wishes. Musk began issuing statements promising that the Roadster would be shipped to customers in early 2008. He also talked of launching a new sedan, which would be priced around $50,000. Tesla started building showrooms for its car.

Now it was the same Musk who had built successful ventures like PayPal and SpaceX. When it came to issues like the faulty carbon-fiber body panels, Musk flew to England to buy new manufacturing tools. Elon got down to do some intense cost-cutting. The employees met every Thursday morning at 7 A.M for bill-of-materials updates. They were required to know the price of every part. The costs of the parts were analysed each month.

Many of the old recruits of the company had begun to leave. But apart from the dwindling workforce, the company had bigger issues to take care of. In 2008, the company began heading towards bankruptcy. The Roadster had cost about $140 million to develop. This was $25 million more than the originally estimated budget. This was an overall tough period for the automobile industry. The big automakers in the country were moving towards bankruptcy. The company was in a desperate need of funds.

❑

The Real Life Iron Man

•

After the Hollywood movie, Iron Man came out; Musk started to become more of a public figure. He enjoyed a rising profile. He soon bought a house in Bel Air. While he was not a regular drinker, he actively took part in the Hollywood nightlife.

It was Musk's wife Justine who relished the newfound status of the couple the most. She maintained a blog detailing the couple's family life. But little did Musk realise that her spouse's blog was soon to turn into one of his worst nightmares.

Tesla became the darling of the press. The reporters tracked its every move and were breathless in their coverage. Musk had started to get very worried about this extravagant coverage by the press that he received. When SpaceX's second launch attempt failed, the reports from the press took a downside. Musk's fortune nearing $200 million was at stake. Press began to gossip about Musk's money problems. In 2007, Valleywag, a gossip blog, started digging into the histories of Zip2 and PayPal. They framed stories about the times Musk was ousted as CEO. The blog named the Tesla its Number 1 failure of the year. It was the time when his triplets—Kai, Damian, and Saxon had joined their brothers Griffin and Xavier. His wife Justine suffered from postpartum depression following the birth of the triplets.

Tesla had to start over on the production of their cars, and SpaceX was awaiting the next launch of the Falcon 1. Both the companies began finishing off Musk's fortune. He had to sell off his possessions like the car McLaren to generate some extra cash. He always encouraged his employees to do their best. He also oversaw important buys at both the companies. His devotion towards Tesla and SpaceX began exacerbating the strains in his marriage. He could not spend much time with his five children. He worked seven days a week. Justine was overwhelmed with his work schedule. Justine longed for Elon, and in her heart, she cherished the time she spent with him during their early days.

On June 16, 2008, Musk filed for divorce. Instead of making the situation public right away, Justine left subtle hints of it on her blog. The gossip magazine Valleywag published a story about the divorce spreading rumours about Musk. In the posts that followed, Justine began writing more liberated versions of how the marriage ended and about the inner workings of the divorce proceedings. It dealt a devastating blow to Musk's public image.

In one of her blogs titled "golddigger", Justine said, she was fighting for a divorce settlement that included their house, alimony, and child support, $6 million in cash, 10 percent of Musk's Tesla stock, 5 percent of Musk's SpaceX stock, and a Tesla Roadster. Later she also appeared on a television show titled Divorce Wars. After the divorce, the couple settled with Justine getting the house, $2 million in cash, $80,000 a month in alimony and child support for seventeen 17 years, and a Tesla Roadster.

The two first filed for divorce in mid-June of 2008. A few months later Elon with one his friends Lee visited the headquarters of Aston Martin to see the company's CEO and get a tour of his factory. On their way back Musk had severe stomach pain. Lee took him to a medical clinic in the middle of a shopping mall. After the pain subsided Lee persuaded Musk into going to a club called Whisky Mist. Musk was escorted into the VIP area. It was there that he met a 22-year-old actress named Talulah Riley. Musk and Riley sat at a table with their friends but immediately zeroed in on each other. It was the first time in weeks that Musk seemed happy. Musk asked Riley for dinner the next night, and unsurprisingly she accepted. Following the dinner Musk and Riley went for a walk and the romance began in sober.

They went on to have lunch the next day and then went to a modern art gallery. After Musk went back to the States, the two kept in touch via e-mail for a couple of weeks, and then Riley booked a flight to Los Angeles. After spending few months with her, Musk wasted no time in asking her for marriage. A stupefied and a flattered Riley accepted his proposal. Soon they started preparing for their marriage. Riley's parents flew to the United States to meet Musk who asked her father for his blessings.

After the sweet stint with the new marriage, Musk had to be back to the harsh realities. Both SpaceX and Tesla were in dire need of cash infusions and with the world's financial markets in disarray, the investments did not seem to be coming. The engineers of his firm remained out on the island, preparing the Falcon 1 for another run. The company had put another group of engineers for the development of Falcon 9. On July 30, 2008, the Falcon 9 had a successful test fire. Three days later, SpaceX test fired Falcon 1. The rocket had an air force satellite as its payload, along with a couple of experiments from NASA. Falcon 1 soared into the sky and flew without any problem. But when the first stage and second stage of the rocket were to separate, there was a malfunction. The second stage of the rocket did not fire properly which was attributed to the fuel-sloshing issues of the rocket.

With the failure of the launch, another one was scheduled. Holding his heart in hands, Musk agreed for the fourth launch. The demands and stakes were insanely high. The body of the rocket had caved in several places. The fuel tank did not stop sloshing. It took two weeks for the rocket to be fixed. The fourth launch was scheduled to take place on September 28, 2008. It was probably to be the final launch of the rocket. The SpaceX team had spent years, separated from their families, battered by the heat, and banished on their petite Launchpad outpost on the island working on the project. The much-awaited day had arrived. In the late afternoon, Falcon 1 was raised into its launch position. It was not carrying real cargo this time but only a 360-pound dummy payload. After the launch button was pressed, the first stage of the rocket fell away. Ninety seconds later the second stage fired up. The engine glowed red and started its six-minute burn. And, lastly, after nine minutes, the Falcon 1 shut down as planned and reached the orbit, becoming the first privately built rocket to attain this feat. The SpaceX team and Musk ruptured into a stream of celebrations.

But celebrations surrounding the victory stonewashed soon as the extent of SpaceX's financial fracas began to occupy the discussions at the boardroom. In the pipeline were the production of Falcon 9 and the construction of Dragon capsule—a machine that could take supplies, and eventually humans, to the International Space Station (ISS). Both the machines were to cost more than $1 billion to complete, an amount that the company could not afford at the moment. Moreover, the company struggled to make its payroll. As 2008 came to an end, Musk had run out of money.

He had to borrow money from his friends. He no longer flew his jet. With a running cost of about $4 million a month, Tesla needed funding to get through 2008. Musk negotiated with investors and sent pleas to anyone with some money to spare. Bill Lee invested $2 million in Tesla, and Sergey Brin invested $500,000. The financial burden was piling up day after day.

In December 2008, NASA was awarding a contract to resupply the space station. The contract was worth of more than $1 billion. Musk was delighted to know that SpaceX was the front-runner for the deal. He began assuring the people responsible for awarding the contract that the company could meet the challenge of getting a capsule to the ISS. For Tesla, Musk went to the existing investors for more funding to avoid bankruptcy. He raised all the personal funds he could and put them into the company. He took out a loan from SpaceX, which NASA approved, and invested that money in Tesla. He also tried to sell some of his shares in Solar City and earned $15 million when Dell took over a data center software start-up called Ever dream, founded by Musk's cousins, in which he had invested.

One of the investors in Tesla, Vantage Point Capital Partners, informed Musk that the firm had a problem with the investment round because it undervalued Tesla. They refused any further investment in the company. Musk feared that Vantage Point would oust him as CEO and emerge as the major owner of the company. Musk now decided to tell the investors that he would take another loan from SpaceX and fund the entire round, all $40 million, himself.

But rumours were doing round in the town that SpaceX had suddenly lost favour with NASA. It was being touted that the space agency would award its contract to another company, but not SpaceX. Proving all such rumours wrong, on December 23, 2008, NASA named SpaceX as the major supplier for the ISS. The company received $1.6 billion as payment for twelve 12 flights to the space station.

Musk broke down in tears on hearing the news. All the pain he had taken till date, all of it seemed worth it.

❑

The Takeoff

After the successful launch, Falcon 9 became SpaceX's workhorse. Nine engines powered it. The company sometimes used the Vandenberg Air Force Base in Southern California to send up Falcon 9 rockets. About four hours before launch, the rocket is filled with liquid oxygen and rocket-grade kerosene. The engineers monitor fuel systems and other items. Ten minutes before launch, they step out of the way and leave the remaining processes up to automated machines. The T-minus-ten-seconds countdown begins. At the count of three, the engines ignite. The computing systems evaluate all nine engines and measure if there's sufficient downward force being produced. At zero the clamps are released. The rocket, with flames surrounding its base, shoots up towards the sky.

In a very short span of time, SpaceX has become one of the most consistent operators of aeronautics industry. It sends rockets to space every month that carry satellites for companies and nations and supplies to the International Space Station. SpaceX beat its competitors like Boeing, Lockheed Martin, Orbital Sciences on every parameter. Moreover, the company produces all of its machines in the United States. Thanks to SpaceX, the United States has remained competitive in the space industry. It's expected that China's role in the space industry will increase, and with the retirement of the space shuttle, the United States has become dependent on the Russians to get astronauts to the ISS. Banking on this opportunity, Russia charges $70 million per person for the trip. SpaceX is the best shot for America to break the Russian hegemony and reliance.

Apart from handling government contracts, the company plans to create a drastic drop in the cost of getting things to space. In coming years, SpaceX plans to cut its price to at least one-tenth that of its rivals. It hopes to take over the majority of the world's commercial launches. SpaceX's reusable rockets and spaceships are the true twenty-first-century machines. The modernisation reflects the company's push to better its technology and alter the fundamentals of the industry.

Musk remains the largest shareholder in the company, which is estimated to be worth $12 billion. Musk aims to bring down the cost of launches to the point that it becomes economical to fly trips to Mars to start a colony.

People describe Musk more as a general than a CEO. He's built on his own an army of engineers, which is best in the game. Musk places emphasis on spotting engineers who ooze passion, and can work as part of a team. The recruiters at SpaceX would hand out blank envelopes to the suitable candidates. The envelope contained an invitation to meet for an initial interview. The candidates that showed up were then subjected to a round of interviews and tests. The potential employees are asked to write an essay for Musk about why they want to work at SpaceX. The final interview takes place with Musk. Each employee is told that Elon will likely keep on writing e-mails and work during the initial part of the interview and not speak much. Don't panic. That's normal. In due course, he will speak to you.

SpaceX's new headquarters in Hawthorne resembles a glacier planted in the middle of Los Angeles. The walls are white. A white table lies in the waiting area. Musk's cubicle is situated on the right side portion of the building. The conference rooms have space-themed names like Apollo or Wernher von Braun. They have photos of a Falcon 1 taking off from Kwaj and the Dragon capsule docking with the ISS.

The SpaceX factory has an area of 550,000-square-foot feet with greyish floors, white walls, and white support columns. Near the entryway, a Dragon capsule hangs from the ceiling. To the left of it is the kitchen, and to the right is a mission control room. It is a closed area having four rows of desks with ten computers each. Around forty 40 feet to the left are Falcon 9 rockets awaiting transport. A data center painted in blue gives it a sci-fi feel. Near the elevators is life-size Iron Man figure.

SpaceX manufactures 80 to 90 percent of its rockets, engines, electronics, and other parts. Whereas its competitors depend on more than 1,200 suppliers. SpaceX buys as little as possible to save money. In addition to building its engines, rocket bodies, and capsules, SpaceX also designs its motherboards and circuits, sensors to detect vibrations, flight computers, and solar panels. To ensure itself, SpaceX sometimes designs a rocket with both the usual gear and prototypes. Engineers then match the performance of the two. Once the SpaceX design equals or outdoes the commercial products, it becomes the de facto hardware. Musk has transferred some of the equipment and techniques of SpaceX to Tesla.

In the early days of SpaceX, Musk was a dynamic software executive trying to learn and understand the worlds of rockets. He initially relied on textbooks to form the bulk of his knowledge. A couple of years later he had turned into an aerospace expert.

The Dragon capsule took SpaceX four years to design, but it is still recorded in the history as the fastest project of such size done in the history of the aerospace industry. Though Dragon looked a lot like Apollo, it had steeper wall angles, to make room for gear and the astronauts. The total cost for Dragon stood at $300 million. Time to time, Musk would send out an e-mail to the whole firm to apply a new policy or to let everyone know about something that's bothering him. The principle at SpaceX is 'to embrace your work and get stuff done.' And to inform Musk that what he's asking is impossible is a big 'no.'

The real difficulty arrives when the SpaceX's work culture and style of functioning go against that of bureaucratic bodies like NASA, the Federal Aviation

Administration, and the U.S. Air Force. The first such difficulty took place on Kwaj when SpaceX wanted to make a change to its launch procedures, but it required a pile of paperwork.

In 2009, SpaceX appointed Ken Bowersox, as its vice president of astronaut safety and mission assurance. Bowersox had a degree in aerospace engineering and also had been a test pilot in the air force. He and Musk were often at odds. Soon Bowersox began to feel like he was being ignored. During one such tussle Musk dismissed Bowersox. Musk has had such rough encounters with high-ranking officials and not been apologetic about it.

Musk's talk like settling on Mars is thrilling and revolutionising space travel amaze people in the aerospace industry. Twenty years after the Wright brothers conducted their experiment, air travel became routine. Space travel, however, has remained a dream for common man. Apart from SpaceX, the American launch providers have inadequate launch capabilities and dubious spirit.

SpaceX's main competitor for ISS resupply missions and commercial satellites in the United States is Orbital Sciences Corporation. Founded in Virginia in 1982, the company focused on putting smaller satellites into low-Earth orbit. Unlike being a true builder like SpaceX, it depends on suppliers, including Russian and Ukrainian companies, for its engines and rocket bodies, making it more of an assembler of spacecraft. And, also it's unable to return experiments and other goods from ISS to Earth.

As for getting humans to space, SpaceX got $2.6 billion from NASA to develop capsules and ferry people to the ISS. The company would be replacing the space shuttle. In June 2010, the Falcon 9 orbited the Earth successfully. In December 2010, SpaceX proved that the Falcon 9 could carry the Dragon capsule into space and that the capsule could be recovered safely after an ocean landing. In May 2012, a Falcon 9 rocket took off from the Kennedy Space Center in Cape Canaveral, Florida. The rocket carried a Dragon capsule to the International Space Station (ISS). With the success of this mission, SpaceX became the only private company to dock with the ISS. Months later the company received $440 million from NASA to keep developing Dragon so that it could transport people. In May 2014, Musk unveiled the Dragon V2, or version two.

Dragon 2 can dock with the ISS without the intervention of a robotic arm. It runs on a Super Draco engine—the first engine built completely by a 3-D printer. Moreover, Dragon 2 can land anywhere on Earth. SpaceX wants to combine three Falcon 9s into a single craft with the ability to carry more than 53 metric tons of weight into orbit. SpaceX is also building a spaceport, which will be able to launch many rockets by automating the processes needed to stand a rocket up on the pad, fuel it, and send it off.

❑

The Rise of Tesla

•

In 2012, Tesla Motors shocked its competitors in the auto industry by launching its Model S sedan - an all-electric luxury car that could cover more than 300 miles on a single charge. It could reach 60 miles per hour in 4.2 seconds and could seat seven people. Moreover, it had two trunks. The car ran on an electric battery pack, which also meant that it ran silently. It scored high on the parameters of speed, mileage, handling, and storage space. And the best part of Model S was its design. It had a 17-inch touch-screen that controlled functions like raising the volume and opening the sunroof. The Model S carried with it an Internet connection. This allowed the driver to stream music using the touch console and use maps for navigation. Instead of turning a key or pushing an ignition button to start the car, driver's weight on the seat did the trick. The car earned the highest safety rating ever. And the fact that it could be recharged for free at Tesla's stations built across the United States made it an economical buy in the long run. The car was an engineering marvel. In comparison to the traditional cars, Model S was about 60 percent more efficient. Tesla sold the Model S directly through its stores and website.

Tesla's stores are modelled on Apple stores. Inside the stores are huge touch-screens where people can calculate how much they can save on fuel costs by switching to an all-electric car. One can also configure the cars on those screens. After the configuration, the customer gives the screen a swipe and his/her Model S appears on a bigger screen in the center of the store. After one places an order, Tesla delivers the car to the given address.

When it comes to the maintenance, there are no oil changes or tune-ups to be dealt with as it does not need any. Though, if something does go wrong with the car, Tesla would come pick it up and repair it. Complaints like the door handle not popping out, windshield wipers not working, etc., are addressed through Internet and software updates. There is also a Smartphone app that allows people turn on air-conditioning or heating and also check where the car was parked on a map. Thanks to regular software updates, the car keeps getting better with time. Soon after the car went on sale, it became one of the most sought-after cars in Silicon Valley. It became the status symbol for wealthy technophiles.

In November 2012, only a few months after the launch, the car was named Motor Trend's Car of the Year. It beat eleven 11 other cars of companies such as Porsche, BMW, etc. Consumer Reports gave the Model S its highest car rating in history—99 out of 100. With such a success Tesla's share price began to soar. One year later, Tesla posted a profit of $562 million.

After the success of Model S, Musk decided to hike the price of its Roadster model to $106,000. Soon Tesla had a safety recall of its Roadster model as it had failed to tighten a bolt properly. The next year, there were reports of a power cable crushing against the body of the Roadster, and it led to short circuits. Hence Tesla had another recall.

In June 2009, Martin Eberhard charged Musk of breach of contract. The lawsuit accused Musk of outdoing his role in Tesla's establishment. But soon he decided to withdraw the suit.

Tesla would make up for its lack of money by hiring people who could outdo the hurdles. Tesla hired engineers, to figure out the inner workings of the Model S. They built an electric Mercedes CLS and used the car to bring investors and partners. To increase the pace of design, engineers worked all day long building the prototype body of the car. To run tests on the body, the car would be loaded up with ballast to represent five people and then make loops around the factory until it overheated or broke down.

The harsh reality lurking before the company was that the odds of Tesla proceeding the Model S to a sellable car were minute. The biggest problem was that it didn't have much money or a factory to mass-produce the cars. They required blanking machines, massive stamping machines, metal dies, and dozens of robots. Such an investment required hundreds of millions of dollars and thousands of workers. Tesla proposed to build a factory first in Albuquerque, New Mexico, and then later in San Jose, California, and then pulled back on these proposals. In January 2009, Tesla took over Porsche's spot at the Detroit auto show. They got the space cheap as other car companies had pulled out of the event. The cars attracted the attention of the big players at the show. After the show, Tesla received an order for four thousand4000 battery packs from Mercedes. In May 2009, Mercedes decided to acquire 10 percent stake in Tesla for $50 million and also signed a deal to have Tesla provide the battery packs. In January 2010, the Department of Energy struck a $465 million loan agreement with Tesla.

Now Tesla had the money to buy a 5.3-million-square-foot feet space to establish a factory. It paid $42 million for the factory. Toyota too decided to invest $50 million in Tesla for a 2.5 percent stake in the company. In the summer of 2010, Tesla started the process of filing for an initial public offering to raise some more capital for its projects. The plan was to raise $200 million through the offering. Performing beyond its expectations, it raised $226 million, and the company's shares went up by more than 41 percent in a day. The IPO stood as the first for an American carmaker since Ford went public in 1956. The money allowed company to expand its engineering teams. It also moved its office from San Mateo to Palo Alto.

The next model in the pipeline was Model X. It was planned to be released as an SUV. It was to be Tesla's merger of an SUV and a minivan built on the Model S foundation. Musk expects the design and technology to be as close to perfect as possible. For him, it has to be either something spectacular with no compromises or nothing. On June 22, 2012, Tesla invited its employees, some customers, and the press to its factory in Fremont. The press and the customers who had never been to the factory before were blown away by their first glimpse of it. The floors, the walls, and the beams were all painted white, while the robots had been painted red.

All this run with success was not to last very long. Multiple roadblocks were awaiting. The biggest of those roadblocks was the fact that the company could only produce about ten sedans in a week. Tesla's stocks became the most shorted stock on the NASDAQ exchange. Amidst all this mayhem, Musk had different goals. He wanted Tesla to become the most profitable major automobile maker in the world. In September 2012, the company unveiled the first leg of a network of charging stations in California, Nevada, and Arizona. Musk planned to construct a worldwide charging network to allow owners recharge quickly and for free. Model S drivers are guided to these stations by the cars' onboard computers.

With huge promises and expectations, Tesla decided to get the Model S to market. Though Tesla did have a large number of reservations, the company struggled to turn them into actual sales. Tesla also lacked finance to revamp its service centers, which were terrible at the time. By the middle of February 2013, the company had fallen into a watershed situation. It immediately required to convert its reservations to purchases or its factory would have gone defunct. This would have cost the company vast amounts of money with the possibility of shares plummeting.

Taking charge of the situation, Musk pulled people from different teams like recruiting, designing, engineering, finance and ordered them to get finish their projects. He then went on a firing spree handing pink slips to senior leaders and promoting junior employees. He then reached out to his friend Larry Page of Google and signed a deal with him regarding Tesla's acquisition by Google. He proposed to remain in control of Tesla for next eight years and $5 billion in capital for factory expansions.

As the two companies discussed the legalities of the deal, a miracle took place. Company's salesmen sold a huge volume of cars in a very short span of time. Tesla posted its first profit, which was a handsome $11 million with $562 million in sales. It managed to deliver 4,900 Model S sedans in few months. This sent Tesla's shares soaring from about $30 a share to $130 per share in July. A few weeks later, it paid off it's $465 million loans to the government. This boosted consumers' confidence. Now the company realised that the deal with Google was no more required. Hence the talks ended. Now Musk held a series of press conferences announcing the construction of more charging stations and the opening of more retail stores.

Tesla's style of functioning is different from other carmakers. Instead of developing new features over a period and then unleashing them in at once, it prefers to update those features to the cars when they're ready. The updates are similarly added to the car as they are on a Smartphone. Tesla users need not go to a gas station either but can charge the cars at their homes. Neither do the cars need oil and transmission fluid changes. With the addition of regenerative braking, the company has managed to extend the life of the brakes. Even its approach to maintenance is different from other carmakers who tend to make huge profits from service.

❑

One Step Further Towards a Green Future

•

The Rive Brothers, apart from being Elon Musk's cousins, their shot to glory was through the company called Ever dream that they founded in the late 1990s. In 2004, brothers Lyndon, Peter and Russ, were in search of something more challenging, something yet unexplored. It was at this time that Musk suggested they to venture into the solar energy market. He was sure of its untapped potential. The brothers took his advice. They went on to spend next two years studying solar technology and the subtleties of the trade. They attended multiple conferences and seminars on solar energy. During one such conference, they stumbled upon the idea of their business model. It was the time when solar panels used to be super expensive to buy. And add to it the cost of installation, it made people reluctant to buy them. The Rives Brothers formed a company called Solar City in 2006. The plan was not to manufacture solar panels but to buy them and install them at the houses. With the help of their software, they analysed customers' past electricity bills and the location of their houses and also how much sunlight they received. Based on all these observations, they used to determine if solar made sense for the property or not. They sent their teams to install the solar panels and ensured that the customer did not pay anything up front for the panels. They allowed customers to lease the panels for a period at a fixed rate. At the end of the lease, the owner could easily move to new, and more effective panels. Musk was the brain behind this model and hence became company's chairman and its largest shareholder.

Years later, the company became the biggest supplier of solar panels in the United States. It also benefited from a fall in the price of solar panels, thanks to the Chinese manufacturers. Even big businesses like Intel, Walgreens, and Wal-Mart signed up for installations. In 2012, when it went public, its shares soared high. In 2014, Solar City was valued at approximately. $7 billion.

In 2014, the company started selling solar energy storage systems built in partnership with Tesla Motors. The Storage systems once charged, could help users get through the night or unexpected power cuts. In June 2014, the company picked up a solar cell maker called Silevo for $200 million. Now instead of buying its solar panels, Solar City would make them at a factory in New York State.

The sky is the limit for Musk. By the end of 2020, he expects to have installed four gigawatts' worth of solar panels, capable of producing five terawatt-hours of electricity per year.

❑

Model X

•

On September 29, 2015, Musk handed out the first Model X car to the customers. The company claims it to be the safest, the quickest, and the most capable sports utility vehicle in history. It has been designed as a family car, loaded with all-wheel drive, ample seating for up to seven adults, standard active safety features, and up to 295 miles of range on a single charge. And it's capable of accelerating from zero 0 to 60 miles per hour in 2.9 seconds.

It has features like eight eight surround cameras for 360-degree vision, twelve 12 ultrasonic sensors for detection of surrounding objects, forward-facing radar to see through heavy rain, fog, dust, and beyond the vehicle ahead—helping to prevent accidents by providing simultaneous visibility in every direction. Model X is the first SUV ever to achieve a 5-star safety rating in every category and sub-category, the lowest probability of occupant injury, and a rollover risk half that of any SUV on the road.

With this car, Elon Musk has fulfilled his promise of providing a greener alternative to the CO2 guzzling traditional cars to an average car buyer. With a price tag of $30,000 and advantages like less refuelling cost and no servicing charges, Model X surely fits in the pocket of an average car owner.

This is another stride of humanity towards a more eco-friendly future, and the credit for it goes to Elon Musk. His name will be inscribed in the pages of history in golden letters.

❑

Musk Says

•

Below is a compilation of Musk's quotes about different aspects of life—

About college: "One particular thing that I learned at Queen's—both from faculty and students—was how to work collaboratively with smart people and make use of the Socratic method to achieve commonality of purpose."

About taking risk: "A failure is an option here. If things are not failing, you are not innovating enough."

About determination: “Optimism, pessimism, f*** that; we’re going to make it happen. As God is my bloody witness, I’m hell-bent on making it work.”

About future: “There’s a fundamental difference, if you look into the future, between a humanity that is a space-faring civilisation, that’s out there exploring the stars … compared with one where we are forever confined to Earth until some eventual extinction event.”

About the purpose of life: “The thing that’s worth doing is trying to improve our understanding of the world and gain a better appreciation of the universe and not to worry too much about there being no meaning. And, you know, try and enjoy yourself. Because, actually, life’s pretty good. It really is.

About Government licensing: “We have essentially no patents in SpaceX. Our primary long-term competition is in China. If we published patents, it would be farcical, because the Chinese would just use them as a recipe book.”

About ideas: “(Physics is) a good framework for thinking. Boil things down to their fundamental truths and reason up from there.”

About hiring: “My biggest mistake is probably) weighing too much on someone’s talent and not someone’s personality. I think it matters whether someone has a good heart."

About perseverance: "If something is important enough, even if the odds are against you, you should still do it."

About ambition: "The first step is to establish that something is possible; then probability will occur."

About kids: "I'm hopeful they will do things like engineering, or write books, or just, in some way, add more than they take from the world."

About progress: "I concluded that we should aspire to increase the scope and scale of human consciousness to understand better what questions to ask. Really, the only thing that makes sense is to strive for greater collective enlightenment."

About his childhood experiments: "It is remarkable how many things you can explode. I'm lucky I have all my fingers."

About iteration: "You want to be extra rigorous about making the best possible thing you can. Find everything that's wrong with it and fix it. Seek negative feedback, particularly from friends."

About motive: "Going from PayPal, I thought: 'Well, what are some of the other problems that are likely to most affect the future of humanity?' Not from the perspective, 'What's the best way to make money?"

About moving fast: "Given that this is the first time in 4.5 billion years where it's been possible for humanity to extend life beyond Earth, it seems like we'd be wise to act while the window was open and not count on the fact it will be open a long time."

❑

Top Motivational Quotes/Inspiring

•

1. A mark of a great man lies in his response to criticism. Don't run away from criticism. Understand it. If it has some truth to it, then fix the problem, and your life or product will improve.
2. A strong sense of purpose makes you persevere when the going gets tough.
3. Actively seek out and listen carefully to negative feedback.
4. America is the spirit of human exploration distilled.

5. As much as possible, avoid hiring MBAs. MBA programs don't teach people how to create companies.
6. As you heat the planet, it's just like boiling a pot.
7. Change is the law of life. And this is good for you. Would you like it if every day was the same? We are here to constantly enhance our experience of life and reach greater heights spiritually, physically, emotionally, and financially. When there is no progress, there is no life.
8. Constantly think about how you could be doing things better and question yourself. I think that's the single best piece of advice.
9. Corner Case can be broken where you can find some corner case in a very unusual circumstance that will break it.
10. Creating a personal and professional culture of optimism and vision is essential for any dynamic and innovative organization.
11. Discover, what your mind is drawn to – movies, painting, singing, writing, engineering, rapping. Pick whatever naturally comes to mind. Work on it for a few months, don't dismiss it outwardly. Then when you have built some skill, take it to the professional level.
12. Do what you want to do. Don't choose a field of work because your friend said something or your parents

said something. Know your talents and abilities, and create something incredible.

13. Don't be afraid of taking risks as long as you take calculated risks. Understand the consequences clearly and learn from people who have walked the same path earlier.
14. Don't delude yourself into thinking somethings working when it's not, or you're going to get fixated on a bad solution.
15. Don't just follow the trend. You may have heard me say that it's good to think regarding the physics approach of first principles. Which is, rather than reasoning by analogy, you boil things down to the most fundamental truths you can imagine, and your reason up from there.
16. Don't worry about the chances of success or failure. Make sure it is possible, and then attack with full force.
17. Each one of us can contribute something – humour, technology, political acumen. You need to discover your potential, your unique talents, and then use them to improve the quality of life for others.
18. Every person in your company is a vector. The sum of all vectors determines your progress.
19. A failure is an option here. If things are not failing, you are not innovating enough.

20. Failure showing up is half the battle. You've got to try hard to do it and don't be afraid of failure.

21. Fear is a hard thing to deal with. I feel it quite strongly. If I think something is important enough, I'll make myself do it despite fear. But it can sap the will. I hate fear; I wish I had it less.

22. Fear is raw, human emotion. Everyone feels it. What matters is whether you run away from it and take a blow to your confidence, or you face it, understand it and then defeat it to strengthen your confidence.

23. For us to have a future that's exciting and inspiring, it has to be one where we're a space-bearing civilization.

24. Fundamentally, if you don't have a compelling product at a compelling price, you don't have a great company.

25. Getting the right people is extremely important. And I interview everyone at SpaceX personally. And were a 500 person company. So that's a lot of interviews.

26. Government isn't that good at rapid advancement of technology. It tends to be better at funding basic research. To have things take off, you've got to have commercial companies do it.

27. Great companies are built on great products.

28. He trails off, as he often does when preoccupied with a thought. Do I try to help: Unethical?

29. I always have optimism, but I'm realistic. It was not with the expectation of great success that I started Tesla or SpaceX. It's just that I thought they were important enough to do anyway.

30. I didn't expect to make any money. If I could make enough to cover the rent and buy some food that would be fine. As it turns out, it turned out to be quite valuable in the end.

31. I think it is a mistake to hire huge numbers of people to get a complicated job done. Numbers will never compensate for talent in getting the right answer (two people who don't know something are no better than one), will tend to slow down progress, and will make the task incredibly expensive.

32. I think that is a mistake and results in a clouded-judgment on important technical issues. They can't tell if something is good or not, so they just do what everyone else does, assuming it to be the safe bet.

33. I think we should be very careful about artificial intelligence. If I had to guess at what our biggest existential threat is, it's probably that. So we need to be very careful. With artificial intelligence, we are summoning the demon.

34. I want to make rockets 100 times, if not 1,000 times better. The ultimate objective is to make humanity a multi-planet species. Thirty years from now, there'll be a base on the moon and Mars, and people will be going back and forth on SpaceX rockets.

35. If humanity is to become multi-planetary, the fundamental breakthrough that needs to occur in rocketry is a rapidly and completely reusable rocket achieving it would be on a par with what the Wright brothers did.

36. If you get up in the morning and think the future is going to be better, it is a bright day. Otherwise, it's not.

37. If your boss is an awful person, you're going to hate coming to work.

38. In this life, we all are creators. You can put a dent in the universe if you try hard and remain loyal to your dreams.

39. It doesn't do a great deal to advance the goal of humanity. I would pay million not to spend six months in Russia. And besides this, my interest is how we enable many other people to go to space, not necessarily me, personally.

40. It doesn't matter how much money you have. You are only as young or as old as your vision and your dreams. If your vision is old and gloomy, you will feel low no matter how much money you have.

41. It has always been my belief that it is our destiny to go beyond our planet and develop sustainable environments elsewhere.

42. It is our destiny to go beyond our planet and develop sustainable environments elsewhere.

43. It was obvious to me that we could never colonize Mars without reusability, any more than America would have been colonized if they had to burn the ships after every trip.

44. It would be an incredible adventure. And life needs to be more than just solving everyday problems. You need to wake up and be excited about the future.

45. We must attempt to extend the life beyond Earth now. It is the first time in the four billion-year history of Earth that it be possible, and that window could be open for a long time – hopefully, it is – or it could be open for a short time. We should err on the side of caution and do something now.

46. It's not about the product you create; it's how you create it. If you create a good product and then stop working hard, your customers will soon be taken by companies who focus on innovation and improving their customer experience.

47. Let's think beyond the normal stuff and have an environment where that sort of thinking is encouraged and rewarded and where it's okay to fail as well. Because when you try new things, you try this idea, that idea well a large number of them are not going to work, and that has to be okay. If every time somebody comes up with an idea it has to be successful, you're not going to get people coming up with ideas.

48. Many things are improbable, only a few are impossible.

49. Many times the hard skills, such as their skills that are needed for the job are much easier to teach and learn that the soft skills needed for teamwork, leadership and influence. Skills can be learned, but intention comes from within. You can't teach or train the heart.

50. My biggest mistake is probably weighing too much on someone's talent and not someone's personality.

51. My motivation for all my companies has been to be involved in something that I thought would have a significant impact on the world.

52. Once you figure out the question, then the answer is relatively easy.

53. One should try to make the world a better place because the inverse makes no sense.

54. One was the Internet, one was clean energy, and one was space.

55. Over time I think we will probably see a closer merger of biological intelligence and digital intelligence.

56. Patience is a virtue, and I'm learning patience. It's a tough lesson. Patience is required because life doesn't change overnight. So be patient, take it one day at a time.

57. People often mistake technology for a static picture. It's less like a picture and more like a movie. It's the velocity of technology innovation that matters. It's the acceleration.

58. People will reject your ideas even when they care for you. So, discover the truths on your own and trust your gut.

59. So many people tried to talk me out of starting a rocket company. One good friend of mine collected a whole series of videos of rockets blowing up and made me watch those. He didn't want me to lose my money.

60. Some people don't like change, but you need to embrace change if the alternative is a disaster.

61. Sometimes the customer doesn't know what they need.

62. Sometimes the media tries to create a more antagonistic position that is the case.

63. Sooner or later, we must expand life beyond our little blue mud ball—or go extinct.

64. Start somewhere and then really be prepared to question your assumptions, fix what you did wrong, and adapt to reality.

65. Start with the basics and build from there. You can't master something by overlooking the fundamentals.

66. Starting and growing a business is as much about the innovation, drive and determination of the people who do it as it is about the product they sell.

67. Stationary storage will be as big as the car business long term. The growth rate will probably be several times what it is for the car business.

68. Talent is extremely important. It's like a sports team, the team that has the best individual player will often win, but then there's a multiplier from how those players work together and the strategy they employ.

69. That's my lesson for taking a vacation: vacation will kill you.

70. The extension of life beyond Earth is the most important thing we can do as a species.

71. The factory is the machine that builds the machine.

72. The fast way is to drop thermonuclear weapons over the poles to warm Mars up to make it hospitable for humans.

73. The finish line is usually a lot further away than you think.

74. The first step is to establish that something is possible then probability will occur.

75. The idea of lying on a beach as my main thing just sounds like the worst — it sounds horrible to me. I would go bonkers. I would have to be on serious drugs. I'd be super-duper bored. I like high intensity.

76. The odds of me coming into the rocket business, not knowing anything about rockets, not having ever built anything, I mean, I would have to be insane if I thought the odds were in my favour.

77. The only reason I was able to accomplish things is the great people willing to work with me.

78. The private sector is very good at organization and innovation.

79. The risk is handsomely rewarded in the business world.

80. The rumours of the demise of the U.S. manufacturing industry are greatly exaggerated.

81. There are some important differences between Tony Stark and me like I have five kids, so I spend more time going to Disneyland than parties.

82. There is an extreme lack of innovation in large industries. I saw it as an opportunity.

83. There's a fundamental difference, if you sort of look into the future, between a humanity that is a space-faring civilization, that's out there exploring the stars compared with one where we are forever confined to Earth until some eventual extinction event.

84. There's a tremendous bias against taking risks. Everyone is trying to optimize their ass-covering.

85. Things of the biggest mistakes we made were trying to automate things that are super easy for a person to do, but super hard for a robot to do.

86. Things You know early in life, I did lots of risky things when I didn't have that much that was depending on me. Now, I have to be more cautious about risky things.

87. To our knowledge, life exists on only one planet, Earth. If something bad happens, it's gone. I think we should establish life on another planet Mars in particular, but we are not making very good progress. SpaceX is intended to make that happen.

88. Understand your emotional nature. If you need some quiet, alone time to recharge, make sure you get some every day. If you like to keep busy, always around people, do that. Do whatever works for you.

89. We need things in life that are exciting and inspiring. It can't just be about solving some awful problem. There have to be reasons to get up in the morning.

90. We need to figure out how to have the things we love, and not destroy the world.

91. We should aspire to increase the scope and scale of human consciousness to understand better what questions to ask.

92. We should create goals that matter to us. What is the one thing you would change about the world? Go work on it, do it, be it, achieve it.

93. When I was in college, I wanted to be involved in things that would change the world. Now I am.

94. When people understand it's done or dies and if we work hard and pull through, it's going to be a great outcome; people will give it everything they've got.

95. When somebody has a breakthrough innovation, it is rarely one little thing. Very rarely, it is one little thing. It's usually a whole bunch of things that collectively amount to a huge innovation.

96. When something is important enough, you do it even if the odds are not in your favour.

97. When you struggle with a problem, that's when you understand it.

98. You can't only look at what an individual employee gets done. You also have to look at how they've helped people around them get things done.

99. You need people who lift your spirits, not the ones you drain your energy and make you want to curl up in your bed.

100. You shouldn't do things differently just because they're different. They need to be better.

❑

Success Principles of Elon Musk

•

Elon Musk is the founder, CEO and chief engineer of SpaceX and the product architect of Tesla Inc. He was the founder of many high calibre start-ups such as PayPal, The Boring Company, Neural ink, Open AI and Zip2. Musk was born on June 28, 1971(age47), to a Canadian mother (Maye Musk) and South African father (Errol Musk).

He was grew up in Pretoria, South Africa. Musk moved to Canada when he was 17 years old, to attend

Queen's University. He received a Bachelor's Degree in Economics from Wharton School and a Bachelor's Degree in Physics from the College of Arts and Sciences. He moved to California in 1995 to begin a PhD in Applied Physics and Material Sciences at Stanford University. Later on, he decided to pursue a business career instead of completing his PhD.

In 2016, Musk was named as one of the "*Top 10 Business Visionaries creating value for the world* "by the Business Insider and ranked at 21st position on the Forbes List of The World's Most Powerful People(2016). In 2019, Musk was listed (co-) first on the Forbes list of the "Most Innovative Leaders".

Today, Elon Musk has become an icon for each one of us. He became a successful person through his hard work and ethics. He is one of the greatest minds who lay a tremendous positive impact on others and inspires us to do something which is out of the box. Musk made us believe in our capabilities. We all have unique skills and mind-sets. It is not essential that you are a follower of someone or you are the leader of your own, your effort and your dedication will decide that you will become a successful person or not. Related to this, let us learn some life enhancing mantras from Elon Musk:

I. "Aspire for the sky with your roots on the ground": Elon Musk Is a man of focus. He aims for the sky without disremembering the significance of the ground. Musk aims for the development of human colonies on the Mars, yet he wants a green and pollution-free earth because he recognises the importance of the planet. He is developing effective technologies day by day to make our earth pollution-free. We must think for a better today, but we should not forget the significance of the past.

II. "Never give up": We all face specific problems in different stages of our life. Elon Musk is a man with a far vision and deals with difficulties smartly with dedication and never gives up. Elon Musk had a very rough childhood. During childhood, his parents divorced, and he decided to live with his father. This turned out to be the worst decision by him, as his father never supported him in any situation and never behaved adequately with him. He faced brutal physical bullying at the school. Sometimes he was beaten up so severely that he has to be hospitalised, but he didn't give up. He was a bright student, and he continued his study and pursued higher education from reputed universities, and now he is an example of success for each one of us. Always remember that there is no taste for success without facing any problem.

III. "Like what you do": Elon Musk was a bright student during his childhood. He loved to read books and keep learning. He was a bookworm and had a scientific interest in modern technologies. He was pursuing his PhD from Stanford University but did not complete it and decided to pursue a business career without thinking about the risks. According to him there is always a chance to fail, and if you are not doing something you like, you will end up quitting the work, and stopping is not a quality of a successful person. We need to recognise our field of interest. Dedication towards anything comes with the driving force of interest. If you don't like what you are doing, you will never be happy, even if you are earning an enormous amount of money.

IV. "Take a risk": Starting a space agency like SPACE X with a considerable investment of money was an immense risk. His friends and family warned Elon Musk for the risk of money loss. But without any effort, there is no success. If you don't trust yourself enough for taking such significant risks, then you would never be able to know about the outcome of it. A person with the courage to take risks deserves success. If you are young, then you should start taking chances because after this period your risk will put an impact on your close ones to whom you are connected emotionally. Now is the time to do that. Start taking risks before you have such obligations. Remember that you are a person with courage, and you will try again if you fail. Try, try, try, then only you will succeed.

V. "Don't listen to little man": In today's world, when a person tries something new or unique, the whole world criticises. No one will encourage you for your decisions except your loved ones. No one wants you to be successful, but your success depends upon the level of your dedication towards your work. When Elon Musk was starting his space agency (SPACE X), one of his friends collected a whole series of videos of rockets blowing up during the launch and made him watch those. He just didn't want Elon to invest such a huge amount into this, but Musk had bigger plans, despite being discouraged by others he choose what he wanted to do and what he liked the most. It was very challenging in the beginning, but now we all are aware of the outcome. We must listen to others and their criticism, but not to discourage ourselves, but to learn from them about our mistakes and should come back even harder.

VI. "Do something important": Whatever you want to do, that work should carry some value or importance. At first, Elon Musk never thought that Tesla would be successful, but he knew that at least they can address the false perception of the people that electric cars had to be ugly, slow and annoying like any other golf car or any other electric car. They came up with the best quality cars in orders to break the misconceptions among the people and to encourage them to buy electric vehicles instead of petroleum fuel cars as they release harmful toxins into the air, degrading the quality of air which we breathe. The importance behind this Tesla product was to tackle the problems which we face due to the toxic fumes of the ordinary petroleum fuel cars. For our mother nature if something is this essential, then you should try that even if the probable outcome is a failure. Never be afraid of failure especially for trying something important. If everyone will think in the same way, then there will be no progress in that particular field. With the help of Tesla, Elon Musk was able to move or shift the automobile industry from fuel cars to electric cars.

VII. "Focus on signal over noise": While investing your resources on something, you must ensure that it guarantees the best outcome from the investment. In Tesla, they never waste money on different types of advertisement. There is no policy for publication in Tesla Inc.; they believe in investing the money in their cars to make the best. Advertisement will only make noise and are less active. An increase in the level of performance of the product will automatically attract buyers. We should never invest our money or any other resource in anything whose return is less like the advertisement in Tesla's example. Always work on the core of your product quality, not on the advertisement of it.

VIII. "Look for problem solvers": Always look for a person who can help you in solving your problems. A person who knows the solution to the issues is considered to be the person who had already gone through that problem. These problem-solvers are experienced and know how to tackle the problem. A person who struggles hard to solve the problem is the person who will help you to become successful, and we should learn from their mistakes. Whenever Elon interviews someone to work at the company, he asks them about the problems they face, if someone is the person who solved the problem, then he would be able to answer the multiple levels, and if not then he/she will be stuck in between. A person with experience will make the situation more comfortable and will help you to solve various problems at different stages. A problem solver is a person who has dedication and concentration towards his/her goals. If a person runs away from the problem instead of solving it, is a person with no quality to become a successful person. Be a brave and intelligent person, and learn to tackle your problems and learn from other problem solvers, what mistakes they make and how often they make mistakes. There's always a story of failure behind a successful person.

IX. "Attract great people": Great people are the people who are talented and hardworking. People who work on their skills rather than getting any specialised degree are great. If you want a job in Tesla or SPACE X, then you have to show your skills rather than your degree. You should make yourself capable of doing several tasks with high power. The person with a degree can fail, but a person with skills will make his/her own to achieve success even after several failures. A company is a group of people, and if you want to become a successful person, you should make a composition of talent and hard work. Elon Musk is a great person because he is talented and hard-working. Musk works for 100 hours in a week. This combination of hard work and talent makes him a high achiever. They are a great source of knowledge, and we can learn many things from them and their experiences.

X. "Have a great product": To become a successful person, you must ensure that you are have higher productivity than any other person. We all work in a particular direction to make our outcomes great. But a successful person will take the outcomes to another level. Elon Musk started two innovative products like SPACE X and Tesla Inc. and ensured that the products are of much higher quality than any other company. According to him, when you enter a pre-settled market, your product must be more excellent than the others, because there must be a reason for the customer to come towards us. Why would anyone buy your product over any other trusted brand?

When Tesla entered the automobile industry, instead of wasting their money on advertisement, they worked hard to make their cars a great product—invested the money on the quality of the product instead of spending the money on an attractive advertisement. A person must ensure that his /her skill of productivity should be higher than any other profession. If you deliver vast productivity, you will get success in return from there.

XI. "Work super hard": If a person wants to achieve something more significant, you must work very hard for that. Nothing is impossible if you're going to make something you lie; you should put all your efforts into that particular thing. When Elon Musk started SpaceX, he didn't have any knowledge about it, but he didn't quit. He worked hard to understand the concepts, he read different books to gain understanding, and the result for this hard work is in front of each one of us. Also, at the time of ZIP2, he and his brother rented an apartment and slept on a couch. There was only one computer, and in the day the website will work, and he did coding through the nights. Even today, he works for 100 hours a week. We have work hard to achieve something more significant. You should never quit your work in the middle. Try, try, try harder, then only you will succeed.

❑